LEADERSHIP IN A CHANGING WORLD

LEADERSHIP

TOUCHING LIVES

LEADERSHIP IN A CHANGING WORLD

Additional books and e-books in this series can be found on Nova's website under the Series tab.

LEADERSHIP IN A CHANGING WORLD

LEADERSHIP

TOUCHING LIVES

CAM CALDWELL

AND

VERL ANDERSON

nova science publishers
New York

NOTICE TO THE READER

Library of Congress Cataloging-in-Publication Data

Names: Caldwell, Cam, author. | Anderson, Verl A. (Verl Allen) author.
Title: Leadership: : touching lives / Cam Caldwell, Verl Anderson.
Description: Hauppauge : Nova Science Publishers, 2020. | Series: Leadership in a changing world | Includes bibliographical references and index.
Identifiers: LCCN 2020008084 (print) | LCCN 2020008085 (ebook) | ISBN 9781536176254 (paperback) | ISBN 9781536176261 (adobe pdf)
Subjects: LCSH: Leadership.
Classification: LCC HD57.7 .C35255 2020 (print) | LCC HD57.7 (ebook) | DDC 658.4/092--dc23
LC record available at https://lccn.loc.gov/2020008084
LC ebook record available at https://lccn.loc.gov/2020008085

Published by Nova Science Publishers, Inc. † New York

CONTENTS

PREFACE

The capacity of a leader to influence the success of an organization – or to fail to achieve that organization's goals – is widely acknowledge by observers of all types. Employees report that their supervisors and managers consistently fail to utilize the potential that those employees not only possess but that they would like to contribute to their organizations. The result of ineffective leaders is that organizations underperform and employees often feel frustrated, unappreciated, and underutilized. The new Gallup research publication, *It's the Manager,* declares the results of their research conducted worldwide about the keys to successful or underperforming organizations.

Leadership is far more than a personal interaction . . . but it is a relationship with others in which a leader makes a significant difference – not only for organizations but for the people who work within them. The message of this book is that each individual can enhance her or his leadership capacity by developing skills and honoring duties to others that are the true heart of leadership. That message of the leader's obligation to serve others has been demonstrated by thousands of leaders who have not only achieved outstanding organizational results but have literally blessed the lives of others as well.

Leaders can also destroy personal commitment, undermine the quality of life of those with whom they work, and fail miserably in their quest to achieve important goals. In addition, leaders can achieve seemingly outstanding organizational results without honoring their obligations to the people with whom they work – and can actually destroy others' quality of life and hamper not only others' individual progress but the long-term course of their lives as well.

We encourage the reader to carefully examine his or her self as (s)he reads the chapters of this book. Leadership is a sacred responsibility, often taken for granted – and often done poorly. We commend to you these chapters and encourage you to not only become your very best self but to serve others with whom you work so that they can achieve their highest potential as well.

Cam Caldwell
Verl Anderson

Chapter 1

LEADERS TOUCH LIVES: INTRODUCTION AND OVERVIEW

Leaders play important roles in our lives and organizations are successful or fail based largely upon the impact of their leaders[1]. Leadership is about achieving results[2] and the consequences of leaders' actions have the potential to reach throughout the globe – and often do It would be naïve and inaccurate to suggest that leadership is not an important issue – or to question whether leaders have left an indelible mark on the world.

Leadership is about **achieving results** and the consequences of leaders' actions have the **potential to reach throughout the globe – and often do.**

---

[1] Collins, J., (2001). *Good to Great: Why Some Companies Make the Leap . . . And Others Don't*. New York: HarperCollins.

[2] This reality has been articulated by many scholars and consultants in describing how leaders ought to be evaluated. See "Peter Drucker Quotes." *AZ Quotes*. Found online on December 27, 2019 at https://www.azquotes.com/author/4147-Peter_Drucker.

Despite the acknowledged importance of leaders, the disappointing reality is that trust in leaders throughout the globe seems to be at its nadir, or lowest point[3]. Whether as heads of government, businesses, the media, colleges and universities, or even in religious organizations, those who lead are often viewed with skepticism, distrust, and even animosity.

Recent Gallup polls indicate, for example, that **more employees worldwide are actively disengaged** – actually working against their own organizations' interests – **than positively engaged**. According to the 2013 survey of **employees in 142 different countries**, 24% of employees were actively disengaged and 63% reported that they were not engaged while only 13% described themselves as positively engaged.

Recent Gallup polls indicate, for example, that more employees worldwide are actively disengaged – actually working against their own organizations' interests – than positively engaged[4]. According to the 2013 survey of employees in 142 different countries, 24% of employees were actively disengaged and 63% reported that they were not engaged while only 13% described themselves as positively engaged[5].

The focus of this chapter is on introducing the important role of leaders and leadership in touching the lives of others – both in positive and in

---

[3] Harrington, M., (2017). "Survey: Peoples Trust has Declined in Business, Media, Government, and NGOs." *Harvard Business Review*, January 16, 2017 and found online on December 27, 2019 at https://hbr.org/2017/01/survey-peoples-trust-has-declined-in-business-media-government-and-ngos.

[4] According to the 2018 Gallup employee engagement survey, only 15% of employees worldwide were positively engaged. The 2013 Gallup survey reported that 24% of employees were actively disengaged.

[5] Crabtree, S., (2013). "Worldwide, 13% of Employees are Engaged at Work." Gallup. October 8, 2013 and found online on December 26, 2019 at https://news.gallup.com/poll/165269/worldwide-employees-engaged-work.aspx.

negative ways. After identifying four important factors associated with leadership, the chapter will then briefly summarize the content of the nine remaining chapters of this book so that readers interested in leadership can identify the areas of leadership of greatest interest to them personally.

Each of the chapters in this book is about one specific element of leadership. The nine remaining chapters identify both positive and negative dimensions of each of those elements and cites real world examples of leaders who personify both ends of that continuum. This chapter then concludes with a challenge to readers to refine and polish their leadership skills so that they can positively affect those individuals and organizations whom they serve.

LEADERSHIP: A PERSONAL RELATIONSHIP

Leadership is a personal relationship that is fully as much related to the heart and soul as it is to the mind[6]. Rather than an arms-length and impersonal association with others, leadership is most effective when the connection is one-on-one and based upon common values. This connection with others demonstrates a leader's ability to care and to be trusted.

Leaders **establish relationships of trust by being trustworthy.** Trust and commitment come from **communicating to others that they truly matter**, and affirming that they are **individually important**, and demonstrating that the **goals of the leader are virtuous.**

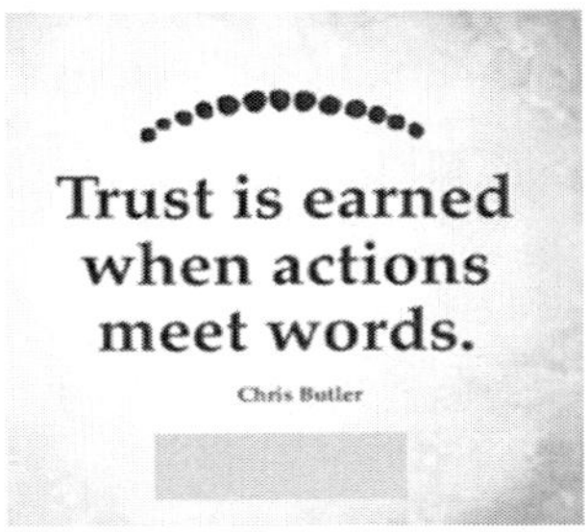

[6] The importance of leadership as it relates to the heart and the mind is clearly enumerated in Kouzes, J. M. & Posner, B. Z. (2017). *The Leadership Challenge: How to Make Extraordinary Things Happen in Organizations*. San Francisco, CA: Jossey-Bass.

Leaders establish relationship of trust by being trustworthy. Trust and commitment come from communicating to others that they truly matter, affirming that they are individually important, and demonstrating that the goals of the leader are virtuous[7]. Although trustworthiness is a subjective perception based upon followers' values, trust in leaders is the key to effective relationships.

Building relationships with people who share a common purpose enables a leader to create relationships that are authentic and genuine[8]. The key to establishing authentic relationships is in recognizing that others are not only essential to accomplishing an organization's purpose but they are of inherent value. Such leaders treat others as ends in and of themselves . . . . and never as means to an organization's goals or a leader's agenda[9]. Wise leaders align themselves with others who share their values, goals, and priorities – recognizing that the success of their combined efforts depends upon that unified purpose.

The key to establishing authentic relationships is **in recognizing that others are not only essential** to accomplishing an organization's purpose but they are **of inherent value.** Such leaders **treat others as ends** in and of themselves . . . .and **never as means to an organization's goals or a leader's agenda.**

In creating relationships with others, inspiring leaders earn followership commitment by demonstrating that they have become the best version of themselves – but are nonetheless still committed to constantly being better.

---

[7] Caldwell, C., Hasan, Z., and Smith, S. 2015. "Virtuous Leadership: Insights for the 21st Century." *Journal of Management Development*. Vol. 34, Iss. 9, pp. 1181-1200.

[8] Atwijuka, S., and Caldwell, C., (2017). "Authentic Leadership and the Ethic of Care." *Journal of Management Development*, Vol. 36, Iss. 8, pp. 1040-1051.

[9] Caldwell, C., Hasan, Z., and Smith, S. (2015). "Virtuous Leadership: Insights for the 21st Century." *Journal of Management Development*. Vol. 34, Iss. 9, pp. 1181-1200.

In addition, trusted leaders also demonstrate their commitment to helping those with whom they work to also become their best. Thus, the leadership relationship is about discovering who we are and who we can become; it is about striving to become better than we are, and helping everything and everyone around us to become better too[10].

Thus, the leadership relationship is about **discovering who we are** and who we can become; it is about **striving to become better** than we are, and **helping everything and everyone around us to become better** too.

LEADERSHIP: MORAL AND ETHICAL RESPONSIBILITY

The brilliant James McGregor Burns reminded us that leadership and ethics are so connected that they are the equivalent to being two sides of the same coin[11]. The moral leader is perceived as responsible when (s)he integrates elements of justice and a commitment to correct principles associated with "Masculine morality" with a caring, responsive, and responsible appreciation of the importance of relationships which characterize "Feminine morality[12]".

---

[10] This reference paraphrases Covey, S. R. (2004). *The 8th Habit: From Effectiveness to Greatness*. New York: Free Press, p. 98 and Daskal, L. "The 100 Best Leadership Quotes of All Time." Found online on December 27, 2019 at https://www.inc.com/lolly-daskal/the-100-best-leadership-quotes-of-all-time.html.

[11] Burns explains throughout his book why Leadership and Ethics are so closely related. See Burns, J. M., (2010). *Leadership*. New York: Harper Perennial.

[12] The integration of these two moral positions is explained in many places. See, for example, Caldwell, C. and Anderson, V., (Eds.) (2019). *Leading with Love*. Hauppage, New York: NOVA Publishing.

The brilliant James McGregor Burns reminded us that **leadership and ethics are so connected** that they are the equivalent to being **two sides of the same coin.**

The ethics scholar, LaRue Hosmer, from the University of Michigan, made it abundantly clear that ethical perspectives are viewed through the subjective lenses of those who perceive the leader's actions[13]. Trust in a leader's moral and ethical compass reflects the follower's alignment with that compass and differences in those priorities result in follower distrust[14].

Leaders who adopt a transformative ethics perspective that integrates many different ethical philosophies are capable of being perceived by followers as both more ethical and more trustworthy than leaders whose ethical perspective is narrow[15].

The moral responsibility of leaders includes the obligation to 1) create **value in the short-term**, 2) create **value in the long-term**, and 3) **do no harm.** Leaders who honor these responsibilities seek to **optimize long-term wealth creation** and are **perceived as ethical stewards** who earn the trust, commitment, and respect of others.

[13] Hosmer addresses the varied perspectives of ethics in several places. See, for example, Hosmer, L. T., (1995). "Trust: The Connecting Link between Organizational Theory and Philosophical Ethics." *Academy of Management Review*, Vol. 20, No. 2, pp. 379-403.

[14] *Ibid.*

[15] Al Lawati, H. A. H., Sayed, R. T., and Caldwell, C., (2019). "Transformative Ethics and Moving Toward 'Greatness.' – Problems and Realities." *Journal of Values-Based Leadership.* Volume XII, Iss. 1, Winter/Spring Edition.

The moral responsibility of leaders includes the obligation to 1) create value in the short-term, 2) create value in the long-term, and 3) do no harm[16]. Honoring these responsibilities optimizes long-term wealth creation and are ethical stewards[17] who earn the trust, commitment, and respect of others[18]. Earning this trust is critical to obtaining the extra-role behavior and personal investment that are often so important to sustaining a competitive advantage[19].

LEADERSHIP: THE MANAGEMENT OF MEANING

Leaders translate worthy goals into reality[20]. The leader's role in defining the direction of an organization is a fundamental responsibility and is a key part of the leader's ability to manage meaning[21]. By providing clear direction and aligning the efforts of an organization, effective leaders assist those with whom they work to stay on track, avoid wasting scarce resources, and optimize their ability to achieve goals.

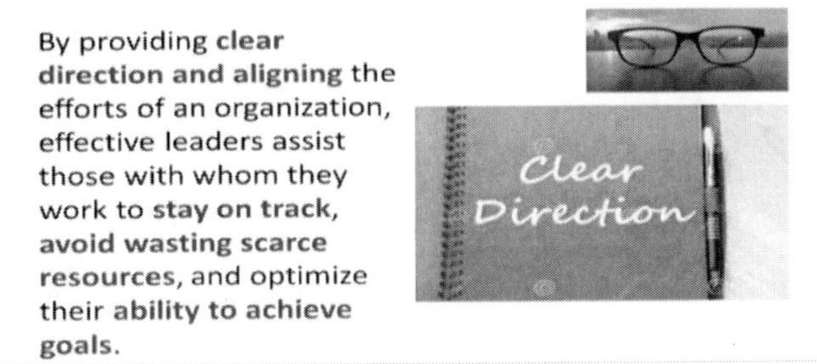

---

[16] Lennick, D. & Kiel, F., (2016). *Moral Intelligence 2.0: Enhancing Business Performance and Leadership Success in Turbulent Times*. Hoboken, NJ: FT Press.

[17] Caldwell, C., Hayes, L., and Long, D., (2010). "Leadership, Trustworthiness, and Ethical Stewardship." *Journal of Business Ethics*, Vol. 96, Iss. 4, pp. 497-512.

[18] Hayes, L., Caldwell, C., Licona, B. and Meyer, T. E., (2015). "Follower Behaviors and Barriers to Wealth Creation." *Journal of Management Development*, Vol. 34, Iss. 3, pp. 270-285.

[19] Caldwell, C. and Anderson, V. (Eds). (2017). *Competitive Advantage: Strategies, Management, and Performance*. 2017. Hauppage, New York: NOVA Publishing.

[20] "Warren G. Bennis Quotes about Leadership." *AZ Quotes*. Found online on December 28, 2019 at https://www.azquotes.com/author/1232-Warren_G_Bennis/tag/leadership.

[21] Burns, J. M., (2010), *op. cit.*

The ability of a leader to identify the objectives of an organization and to provide a point of reference for others about the goals to be accomplished are essential in convincing others to support those outcomes[22]. Thus, this management of meaning enhances the process by which leaders earn the followership of others[23].

The leadership role defines the strategy and structure of an organization, identifies the key roles played by team members, articulates policies and practices that frame the organization's control systems, and coordinates the acquisition of resources required for an organization to function as it seeks to achieve its goals[24]. Each of these responsibilities is essential for an organization to survive over the long term – and each of them provides clarity and direction for team members as they, in turn, carry out their individual roles[25]. It is by framing and providing meaning to the context in which an organization operates that leaders communicate what is needed for their team members to integrate their efforts[26].

It is by **framing and providing meaning** to the **context in which an organization operates** that leaders **communicate what is needed** for their team members to **integrate their efforts.**

As important as their framing and directing roles, leaders manage meaning by giving purpose to the efforts being performed by their

[22] Smircich, L. & Morgan, (1982). 'Leadership: The Management of Meaning." *Journal of Applied Behavioral Science*, Vol. 18, No. 3, pp. 257-273.

[23] *Ibid.*

[24] *Ibid.*

[25] *Ibid.*

[26] *Ibid.*

colleagues. By communicating the reason and purpose behind what is being accomplished and by translating individual tasks into worthy goals and objectives, leaders manage meaning that does more than simply explain what is needed to be done. The Canadian author and philosopher, Matshona Dhliwayo, explained the leadership relationship as follows[27].

> When you touch minds, people are willing to walk a dozen miles for you; and when you touch hearts, people are willing to walk a thousand miles for you; but when you touch souls, people are willing to walk a million miles for you.

It is this ability to connect with others that gives real meaning to what leaders are seeking to accomplish.

LEADERSHIP: COMMON PRACTICES

In their best-selling book, *The Leadership Challenge*, James Kouzes and Barry Posner identified five common practices that they identified as important contributors to success as leaders serve others[28].

- *Model the Way*
  Effective leaders clarify shared values and set the example by their actions. What they do is consistent with what they ask others to do. By living their values and by teaching others how to conform with those same values, leaders strengthen an organization.
- *Challenge the Process*
  Leaders ask appropriate questions about why organization tasks are performed in traditional ways. They search for opportunities to improve an organization and are willing to introduce better ways to

---

[27] "Lead Quotes Quotes." *GoodReads* found online on December 27, 2019 at https://www.goodreads.com/quotes/tag/lead-quotes.

[28] Kouzes, J. M. & Posner, B. Z., (2017). *The Leadership Challenge: How to Make Extraordinary Things Happen in Organizations* (6th ed.). San Francisco, CA: Jossey-Bass.

achieve goals. Leaders take well-reasoned risks and experiment when opportunities arise to improve the organization.

- *Inspire a Shared Vision*

  Leaders enlist others in the pursuit of a valued purpose and provide clear direction about worthy outcomes to achieve. They provide a well-defined perspective about what is possible in a way that is in harmony with shared values and ideals.

- *Enable Others to Act*

  By providing the resources and operational policies that guide employees, leaders facilitate accomplishing important tasks and guide needed changes. By establishing strong relationships, they create a climate of trust and build the confidence and competence of individual members.

- *Encourage the Heart*

  Leaders recognize the contributions of others and establish personal connection with team members. They create a spirit of community and cooperation and establish an organization culture that supports shared effort and the alignment of values.

Each of these five practices enables a leader to more effectively serve the organization, contribute to the achievement of shared goals, and benefit an organization's participants.

SUMMARIZING THE CHAPTERS

The nine remaining chapters of this book are summarized below. Each chapter identifies important ways in which leaders are able to profoundly influence their team members and organizations. In each chapter, the clear message is that the qualities of leadership described make a significant difference in whether an organization is successful in accomplishing its goals or contributes to organizational failure.

Chapter 2 – Moral Leadership or the Leader as Steward

The purpose of this chapter is to examine the complex nature of moral leadership and the role of the leader as an ethical steward. After identifying the high standards of stewardship, the chapter then identifies the characteristics of organizational leaders who seem to lack this vital leadership quality. Citing the example of S. Truett, Cathy, founder of the highly successful Chick-fil-A chain of restaurants, the chapter describes Cathy's fit with the criteria of the highly ethical steward. Cathy is then contrasted with a once highly-regarded but now largely discredited leader who not only does not fit the ethical stewardship profile but has been repudiated for his violation of moral, ethical, and legal principles. After identifying five qualities of ethical stewardship that today's leaders should consider adopting, the chapter ends with encouragement to leaders who seek to be perceived as both moral and ethical.

Chapter 3 – Leaders Prepare for Change

The purpose of this chapter is to identify the factors that are vital to lead individuals and organizations in the change process. After identifying those key variables, the barriers to change that leaders face are then described. The leadership role of Darwin Smith, Chief Executive Officer (CEO), in guiding the change at Kimberly-Clark is cited as an example of a leader who successfully coordinated the change process. His success is contrasted with that of the failure of the leader of a major department store CEO in its financial decline. Five important factors are identified insights for leaders to remember as they address the pressures of change. The chapter concludes with encouragement to leaders as they prepare for constant change.

Chapter 4 – Integrity and Its Consequences

The focus of this chapter is on explaining the significance of integrity as a leadership quality and to present two contrasting examples of leaders. One leader has been known for his great integrity. The lack of personal integrity of the other leader resulted in his personal disgrace, the loss of millions of investor dollars, and the individual ultimately being sent to jail for financial fraud. The chapter begins by defining identity, based upon the insights of several scholars. It then identifies five important characteristics of integrity and contrasts those characteristics with the qualities of individuals who lack integrity.

Chapter 5 – Honoring Others Kindness, Trust, and Leadership

The focus of this chapter is on explaining the nature of kindness as a leadership quality that transcends simply treating others with dignity and respect – although that element of kindness is also important. In today's world of arms-length employer-employee relationships, leaders who are kind set the tone for their entire organization and, by so doing, they create an organizational culture that breeds high trust and commitment.

Chapter 6 – Leadership and Generosity

The focus of this chapter is on the precise nature of generosity as a leadership quality. The chapter begins by defining generosity and citing six ways in which a leader's generosity positively influences others in organizations. The chapter then contrasts personal generosity with greed – the antithesis of a generous heart. Citing the inspiring example of David Packard, the co-founder with William Hewlett of the multinational information technology company that bears their names, the chapter briefly describes Packard's personal example of leadership and the generosity throughout his life for which he was known.

Chapter 7 – Feminine Leadership and Its Strengths

The purpose of this chapter is to examine the advantages of the feminine leadership style, acknowledging in advance that there is no definitive leadership approach that applies to every woman. Acknowledging that there is often as much or more difference in leadership characteristics among women than there is between men and women, this chapter identifies general tendencies about the leadership approach that categorizes the interpersonal style of many women who serve in leadership positions.

Chapter 8 – Leadership and Responsibility

The purpose of this chapter is to address the importance of social responsibility as a leadership obligation. The chapter begins by briefly summarizing five theories of organizational governance and distinguishing their varying perspectives about the leader's role. After providing this overview, the chapter then describes the actions of two different leaders. One of those leaders is Muhammud Yunus, a social entrepreneur and the founder of the Grameen Bank who was ultimately awarded the Nobel Prize for his service to others. The other leader was Chief Executive Officer of one of the world's most successful corporations whose company polluted a major U.S. river and who served at the company's helm while it delayed the clean-up of that river for two decades. The chapter concludes with four recommendations for leaders regarding their role in guiding the social responsibility of their companies.

Chapter 9 – Leaders Develop People

The focus of this chapter is on the vital role of leaders in serving others, developing others' capacity as leaders themselves, and utilizing those skills to effectively benefit their organizations. The chapter begins by identifying seven important ways in which effective leaders are able to develop the abilities of those with whom they work. Following that introduction, the chapter contrasts the success of Max DePree, former Chief Executive Officer of Herman Miller Furniture, with the ineffective outcomes of a school administrator who treated his staff and faculty like commodities and ended up achieving far less for his college and his students than was easily achievable.

Chapter 10 – Leadership as Service to Mankind

The purpose of this chapter is to identify the important role of service and its importance in influencing the lives of others. The chapter begins by identifying the importance of service as a fundamental quality of great leadership. Following that summary, the chapter then identifies the consequences when leaders choose self-interest over service to others and the impacts of that choice. The chapter then describes the commitment to others and dedicated service of Dr. Roy Vagelos, former Chief Executive Officer and Chairman of Merck, Co. who was responsible for Merck developing and donating Ivermectin, a drug that cured river blindness for millions of impoverished people in the third world.

CONCLUSION

The goal of leadership is to become the type of leader that others would voluntarily follow, even if the person leading had neither formal title nor position[29]. Great leaders are valued by others in direct proportion to the number of lives that they have touched for the better[30]. For each leader, or for those who desire to lead, greatness is ultimately achieved by finding a purpose for their lives and then living their life for that purpose[31].

Great leaders are valued by others in **direct proportion to the number of lives** that they have **touched for the better.** For each leader, or for those who desire to lead, **greatness is ultimately achieved by finding a purpose** for their lives and then **living their life for that purpose.**

The noted Indian poet, Avijeet Das, has reminded us that money will not last and fame will not last -- but how we have touched others will always stay behind! It is by touching lives, by helping others to discover the greatness that lies within them, and by enabling organizations to accomplish a worthy objective that leaders fulfill their highest purpose. It is ultimately the challenge that each individual has in his or her life to touch the lives of others in positive ways. In pursuit of that challenge each one of us possesses an exciting opportunity.

---

[29] Daskal, L., "The 100 Best Leadership Quotes of All Time." *Inc.* Found online on December 28, 2019 at https://www.inc.com/lolly-daskal/the-100-best-leadership-quotes-of-all-time.html. This is a paraphrase of a quote by Brian Tracy.

[30] *Ibid.* This quote comes from Vishwas Chavan, *Vishwasutras: Universal Principles for Living: Inspired by Real-Life Experiences.*

[31] *Ibid.* This is a paraphrase of a quote from Avijeet Das.

It is by **touching lives, by helping others to discover the greatness** that lies within them, and by **enabling organizations to accomplish a worthy purpose** that leaders will fulfill their highest purpose. It is ultimately **the challenge that each individual has in his or her life to touch the lives of others** in positive ways.

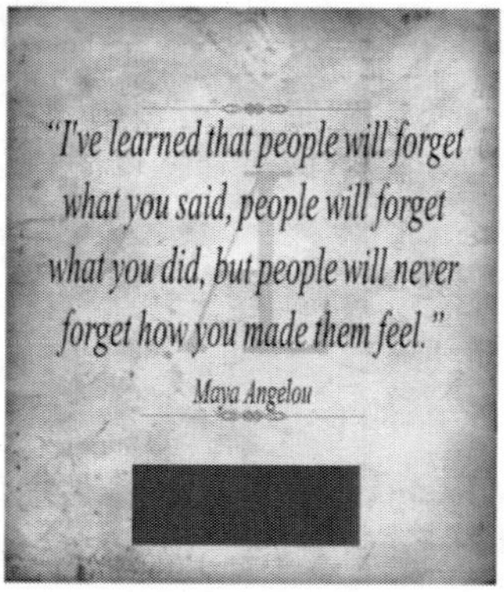

Chapter 2

MORAL LEADERSHIP OR THE LEADER AS STEWARD

The role of the leader and the duties which (s)he owes others has been the source of a multitude of books, articles, and essays – and is a source of great interest in government, non-governmental organizations, academic institutions, and business organizations.

Recent research confirms not only that **trust in leaders has substantially diminished** but that **organizational success or failure is highly leader dependent.** Almost without exception, that trust is closely tied to followers' **perceptions about the moral leadership** of those who lead them.

Recent research confirms not only that trust in leaders has substantially diminished[32] but that organizational success or failure is highly leader dependent[33]. Almost without exception, that trust is closely tied to followers' perceptions about the moral leadership of those who lead them.

The clear evidence is that people leave leaders and supervisors rather than organizations – often because "bosses" fail to 1) invest in their employees, 2) fully engage them in their work, and 3) listen effectively to their expressed needs.[34] The feeling of employees is that their managers and supervisors have violated the implicit psychological contract owed to them and that, in failing to honor that contract, their leaders have failed to honor the stewardship obligations of a moral leader[35].

The feeling of employees is that their **managers and supervisors have violated the implicit psychological contract** owed to them and that, in failing to honor that contract, their leaders have **failed to honor the stewardship obligations** of a moral leader.

The purpose of this chapter is to examine the complex nature of moral leadership and the role of the leader as an ethical steward. After identifying the high standards of stewardship, the chapter then identifies the characteristics of organizational leaders who seem to lack this vital

---

[32] Harrington, M., (2017). "Survey: People's Trust Has Declined in Business, Media, Government, and NGOs." *Harvard Business Review*, January 16, 2017.

[33] Clifton, J. & Harter, J., (2019). *It's the Manager: Gallup Finds the Quality of Managers and Team Leaders is the Single Biggest Factor in Your Organization's Long-Term Success*. Omaha, NE: Gallup Press.

[34] Goler, L, Gale, J., Harrington, B. & Grant A., (2018). "Why People Really Quit Their Jobs." Harvard Business Review, January 11, 2018, and found online on December 15, 2019 at https://hbr.org/2018/01/why-people-really-quit-their-jobs.

[35] The moral nature of the leader's obligation and the nature of psychological contracts Is clearly addressed in Rousseau, D. M., (1995). *Psychological Contracts in Organizations: Understanding Written and Unwritten Agreements*. Thousand Oaks, CA: Sage Publications.

leadership quality. Citing the example of S. Truett, Cathy, founder of the highly successful Chick-fil-A chain of restaurants, the chapter describes Cathy's fit with the criteria of the highly ethical steward. Cathy is then contrasted with a once highly-regarded but now largely discredited leader who has been discredited for his violation of moral, ethical, and legal principles. After identifying five qualities of ethical stewardship that today's leaders should consider adopting, the chapter ends with encouragement to leaders.

ETHICAL STEWARDSHIP AS VIRTUOUS LEADERSHIP

Stewardship is the responsibility to protect the interests of others for the collective good[36] and is others-directed and long-term in focus[37]. Stewardship behavior on the part of leaders demonstrates the leader's commitment to individual relationships as well as a commitment to the best interests of the larger organization. Stewards are driven by their moral responsibility, based upon a sense of intrinsic commitment to high ideals and their own sense of self-efficacy and self-determination[38].

Stewardship behavior on the part of leaders demonstrates the leader's commitment to individual relationships as well as a commitment to the best interests of the larger organization. Stewards are driven by their moral responsibility, based upon a sense of their sense of intrinsic commitment to high ideals and their own sense of self-efficacy and self-determination.

---

[36] Hernandez, M., (2008). "Promoting Stewardship Behavior in Organizations: A Leadership Model." *Journal of Business Ethics*, Vol. 80, Iss. 1, pp. 121-128.

[37] See Senge, P. M., (2006). The Fifth Discipline: The Art & Practice of the Learning Organization (2nd ed.). New York: Doubleday.

[38] Davis, J. H., Schoorman, F. D. & Donaldson, L., (1997). "Toward a Stewardship Theory of Management." *Academy of Management Review*, Vol. 22, Iss. 1, pp. 20-47.

Ethical stewardship is a leadership commitment that "integrates long-term wealth creation, a commitment to the transformational interests of stakeholders, and creating organizational systems that reinforce both instrumental and normative organizational goals[39]." Covenantal in its focus, ethical stewards honor the sacred nature of leadership and view their responsibilities as "truly investing in and affirming the identities of those whom they serve[40]." By their commitment to organizational values, to the needs of others, and to ensure long-term value creation, ethical stewards connect with others on a heart-to-heart level and earn authentic trust[41].

The underlying **values of the ethical steward** include the virtues of **humility and love**. Leaders with those qualities look for **the good in others** and help them to grow. Ethical stewards **focus on improvement** rather than on others' mistakes.

The underlying values of the ethical steward include the virtues of humility and love[42]. Leaders with those qualities look for the good in others and help others to grow. Ethical stewards focus on improvement rather than on others' mistakes. They have genuine love for others, coupled with the humility to recognize that no one – including themselves – is perfect. As leaders, ethical stewards seek to help others to grow so that each individual and the entire organization can benefit thereby[43].

---

[39] See page 153 of Caldwell, C., Hayes, L., Karri, R., and Bernal, P., (2008). "Ethical Stewardship: Implications for Leadership and Trust." *Journal of Business Ethics*, Vol. 78, Iss. 1/2, pp. 153-164.

[40] *Ibid*. See p. 157.

[41] *Ibid*.

[42] Okpala, C. O. & Caldwell, C. (2019). "Humility, Forgiveness, and Love: The Heart of Ethical Stewardship." *Journal of Values-Based Leadership*, Vol. 12 Summer 2019 and found online at https://scholar.valpo.edu/jvbl/vol12/iss2/10/

[43] *Ibid*.

Ethical stewards are **committed to the welfare of others,** treat their colleagues so well that others **come to recognize the best versions of themselves,** and strive to also **achieve their own highest potential.**

Ethical stewards affirm the value and identity of individuals while demonstrating their commitment to the long-term interests of the entire organization[44]. By seeking to optimize outcomes, being value-based, and principle-centered, leaders who are stewards demonstrate their trustworthiness by their actions. Ethical stewards are committed to the welfare of others, treat their colleagues so well that others come to recognize the best versions of themselves, and strive to achieve their own highest potential[45].

LEADERS AND SELF-INTEREST

Leaders who lack a stewardship perspective tend to pursue self-interest with guile.[46] Adopting a "What's in it for me?" perspective, such leaders view others as a means to their personal benefit and look upon the organization's success as a reflection of their own value.

---

[44]Caldwell, C., Hayes, L., Karri, R., and Bernal, P., (2008), *op. cit.*

[45] See Covey's definition of leadership on pages 98 and 99 of Covey, S. R., (2004). *The 8th Habit: From Effectiveness to Greatness*. New York: Free Press.

[46] The distinction between the leader as steward and the leader as someone who pursues his or her own self-interest is a key theme of Peter Block. See Block, P., (2013). *Stewardship: Choosing Service Over Self-Interest*. San Francisco, CA: Jossey-Bass.

The task of such leaders is to pursue organizational profits and to promote themselves in order to accomplish their own personal agenda. Employees are often viewed as "Its" rather than as "Yous" and the relationships that they establish are typically arms-length and impersonal – except when establishing personal connection is perceived to be in their own self-interest[47].

The task of such leaders is to pursue organizational profits and to **promote themselves in order to accomplish their own personal agenda.** Employees are often viewed as **"Its" rather than as "Yous"** and the relationships that they establish are typically **arms-length and impersonal** – except when establishing personal connection is **perceived to be in their own self-interest.**

On the continuum of virtuous leadership, shown as Figure 1, leaders pursuing self-interest adopt a position that optimizes their own short-term benefit, as compared to the ethical steward's interest in pursuing a long-term virtuous outcome that benefits all stakeholders and optimizes long-term value[48]. Acting with self-interest in mind, leaders who lack a virtuous commitment may make decisions based upon an Ethic of Self-Interest – choosing the best outcome for themselves, rather than basing moral decision-making on principles, values, or the interests of the organization.

---

[47] Caldwell, C., Atwijuka, S., & Okpala, C. O. (2018). "Compassionate Leadership in an Arms-Length World." *Journal of Business and Management.*

[48] Caldwell, C., Hasan, Z., and Smith, S. (2015). "Virtuous Leadership: Insights for the 21st Century." *Journal of Management Development.* Vol. 34, Iss. 9, pp. 1181-1200.

Virtuous	Moral	Amoral	Immoral
Seeks to optimize long-term value creation and magnified duties owed to all stakeholders	Adds value, keeps commitments to stakeholders and society, and obeys laws	Avoids breaking the law, but may act with short-term self-interest rather than that of others	Seek outcomes that maximize perceived self-interest and avoid self-harm

Figure 1. The virtuous leadership continuum.

Leaders who adopt this philosophy of doing what is best for themselves tend to be viewed with great skepticism and distrust by others. Over time, those who work with such individuals recognize that their leader will tend to make choices based upon a situationally contextual set of priorities.

Over time, **those who work with such individuals** recognize that their leader will tend to make **choices based upon a situationally contextual set of priorities.** The welfare of others, according to those priorities, is important if and **only if others' best interests are aligned with the agenda which the leader perceives to be in his/her own interests as well.**

The welfare of others, according to those priorities, is important if and only if others' best interests are aligned with the agenda which the leader perceives to be in his/her own interests as well. Commitment to such leaders is often based upon a belief that compliance is necessary to simply survive or to benefit personally. Otherwise, trust in such leaders ceases to exist – beyond believing that the leader will act for the corporate good only so far as doing so will benefit him/her personally.

The contrast between the moral commitment, the actions, and the intentions of the leader who is an ethical steward and the leader who pursues his or her own self-interests is stark and quickly identifiable in organizations. Unfortunately, many employees perceive that they work in organizations wherein they are viewed as commodities, rather than as valued partners. In a world where employees are treated as commodities, they quickly recognize what their leaders really value.

Many employees perceive that they work in organizations wherein they are viewed as **commodities, rather than as valued partners.** Although the **corporate value statement on the walls of many organizations may state** that their employees are highly valued, **the actions of those who lead tend to convey a distinctly different set of beliefs** – undermining organizational commitment, ownership, and trust on the part of employees.

Although the corporate value statement on the walls of many organizations may state that their employees are highly valued, the actions of those who lead tend to convey a distinctly different set of beliefs – undermining organizational commitment, ownership, and trust on the part of employees. Lacking that commitment and willingness to go the extra mile, organizations underperform and struggle to maintain a competitive advantage[49].

[49] Caldwell, C. and Anderson, V. (Eds). 2017. *Competitive Advantage: Strategies, Management, and Performance*. 2017. Hauppage, New York: NOVA Publishing.

S. TRUETT CATHY – ETHICAL STEWARD

S. Truett Cathy, founder of Chick-fil-A, opened a small restaurant, **The Dwarf Grill, in an Atlanta suburb in 1946.** The family-owned restaurant served a menu that largely consisted of fried chicken. A devout individual, **Cathy believed in running his business according to the way that he tried to order his life.**

S. Truett Cathy

S. Truett Cathy, founder of Chick-fil-A, opened a small restaurant, The Dwarf Grill, in an Atlanta suburb in 1946. The family-owned restaurant served a menu that largely consisted of fried chicken. A devout individual, Cathy believed in running his business according to the way that he tried to order his life. Cathy's chain of restaurants, which he began franchising in 1967, has grown to an empire doing $10 billion in annual sales[50], but is also known for its outstanding customer service, the quality of its products, and the leadership values that Cathy has consistently espoused[51].

More than simply refusing to open its doors on Sundays in order to give its employees a day of rest and to comply his business with his Christian principles. Cathy adopted principles for governing his business based upon seven guidelines "that will work in making a living and in building a life" that he constantly demonstrated[52].

---

[50] Lock, S., (2019). "System Sales of Chick-fil-A in the United States from 2016 to 2018."*Statista*, August 13, 2019 and found online on December 16, 2019 at https://www.statista.com/statistics/743343/system-sales-of-chick-fil-a/.

[51] Maze., J., (2018). "When It Comes to Reputation, Chick-fil-A is King." *Restaurant Business Online*, March 22, 2018 and found online on December 16, 2019 at https://www.restaurantbusinessonline.com/marketing/when-it-comes-reputation-chick-fil-king

[52] These seven principles come from "7 Life Lessons from Truett Cathy." *Dave Ramsey.com* found online on December 16, 2019 at https://www.daveramsey.com/blog/7-life-lessons-from-truett-cathy.

1. Define Your Values and Stick to Them

Cathy made his Christian beliefs the center of his business. His company's mantra has been "To glorify God by being a faithful steward of all that is entrusted to us and to have a positive influence on all who come into contact with Chick-fil-A."

Cathy's **company mantra** has been ***"To glorify God by being a faithful steward of all that is entrusted to us and to have a positive influence on all who come into contact with Chick-fil-A."***

Corporate Purpose

To glorify God by being a faithful steward of all that is entrusted to us and to have a positive influence on all who come into contact with Chick-fil-A

2. A Little Customer Service Goes a Long Way

Chick-fil-A's response, "It's my pleasure," is heard from all of its employees and for Cathy chicken was simply the means by which he accomplished his true purpose: honoring God and helping people.

Chick-fil-A's response, ***"It's my pleasure,"*** is heard from all of its employees and for **Cathy chicken was simply the means by which he accomplished his true purpose**: honoring God and helping people.

Thank you.

My pleasure

3. Make Family a Priority

Chick-fil-A restaurants periodically sponsor special family activities for customers and his "closed on Sundays" philosophy was intended to allow employees to spend time with their own families. Cathy's company remains family run as well.

Chick-fil-A restaurants periodically sponsor **special family activities for customers** and his **"closed on Sundays"** philosophy was intended to **allow employees to spend time with their own families.**

4. Know Why You Exist

The company mantra reinforces for Chick-fil-A its primary purpose. Its focus is not just on chicken, but is on serving people and serving God.

Cathy consciously **sought to prepare and to involve his family in his business.** His intent in doing so was to **extend his legacy** beyond his own life.

5. Plan Ahead

Cathy consciously sought to prepare and to involve his family in his business. His intent in doing so was to extend his legacy beyond his own life.

6. Invest in Others

Chick-fil-A has sponsored the Win Shape Foundation, funded scholarships for its employees, sponsored summer camps for children, and provided long-term foster care for children.

Chick-fil-A has sponsored the **Win Shape Foundation**, funded **scholarships** for its employees, sponsored **summer camps** for children, and provided long-term **foster care** for children.

Chick-fil-A

WinShape Foundation

7. Don't Be Afraid to Start Small

From its early beginnings in the Dwarf Grill in 1946, Chick-fil-A has grown to become a company with more than 2,300 restaurants.

Although Cathy passed away in 2014, **his legacy has continued to grow** and he and his company have **been a superb example of quality of service, quality of products, and ethical leadership**

In every sense, S. Truett Cathy's values and principles mirrored the standards of the ethical steward. Although Cathy passed away in 2014, his legacy has continued to grow and he and his company have been a superb example of quality of service, quality of products, and ethical leadership.

LEADERSHIP WITH SELF-INTEREST

A disappointing contrast of self-serving leadership is the example of an individual who proudly advocated the philosophy, "Mean Business." Believing that the term meant far more than to be firm and resolute, this individual dealt with people and organizations as if they were simply commodities to use to generate the greatest possible profits for himself and for those owners who hired him to "rescue" their companies and generate short-term paper profits. His well-documented "slash and cut" approach to terminating employees to artificially improve the short-term bottom line was legendary and caused him to be nicknamed after a piece of equipment known for its destructive power.

Believing that "Mean Business" meant far more than to be firm and resolute, this individual dealt with people and organizations as if they were simply commodities to use to generate the greatest possible profits for himself and for those owners who hired him to "rescue" their companies and generate short-term paper profits.

A QUICK BUCK APPROACH

Known as a "hired gun," this "CEO for Hire" took pride in his ability to terminate thousands of employees in the name of efficiency and cost-cutting. His name became a byword in the corporate verbiage for "turning around" a company – although the companies he allegedly saved never seemed to recover in the long term. This executive was also known for a "smoke and mirrors" approach to corporate accounting, with his staff frequently being told to "back into a number" that this executive wished to see on his companies' corporate balance sheet.

This executive was also known for a "smoke and mirrors" approach to corporate accounting, with his staff frequently being told to "back into a number" that this executive wished to see on his companies' corporate balance sheet.

Eventually terminated from one company he was called in to "fix" for his accounting machinations, this individual was said to have been guilty of multiple counts of financial fraud allegations throughout his career. Eventually, he settled a claim with the Securities and Exchange Commission for $500,000 and was permanently barred from thereafter serving as an officer or director of a publicly-traded company thereafter. One of his biographers described him as stealing the dignity, purpose, and life out of organizations – replacing them with a management style typified by intimidation and fear.

One of his biographers described him as **stealing the dignity, purpose, and life** out of organizations – replacing them with a **management style typified by intimidation and fear.**

Organizational Terrorist

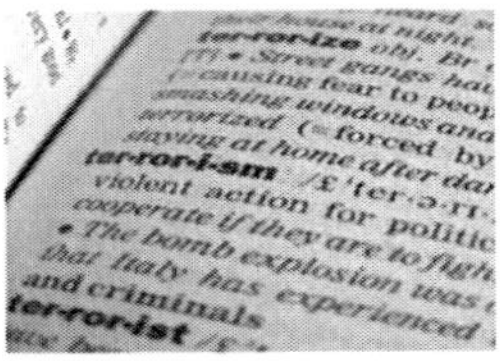

Unfortunately, the "lean and mean" management approach typified by universal corporate downsizing has rarely produced added value or long-term profits in the companies where that approach has been implemented[53]. The false principles of treating people like chattel apparently continue to be in vogue in many organizations – including universities, NGOs, and government and demonstrate that the ethic of self-serving leadership continues to reign as the philosophy of choice in many organizations[54].

The **false principles of treating people like chattel** apparently continue to be **in vogue in many organizations** – including universities, NGOs, and government and **demonstrate that the ethic of self-serving leadership continues to reign as the philosophy of choice** in many organizations.

---

[53] Pfeffer, J., (1998). *The Human Equation: Building Profit by Putting People First*. Boston, MA: Harvard Business Review Press.

[54] Harrington, M., (2017), *op. cit.*

RECOMMENDATIONS ABOUT STEWARDSHIP

Being an ethical steward and honoring the responsibilities of leadership are obligations rarely fully understood by many of today's leaders and managers[55]. Conventional management philosophies and assumptions about what works in business are often archaic and fail to address the demands of an economy that is dependent upon high commitment to achieve high performance[56].

Despite the growing body of evidence about the importance of ethical leadership, leaders struggle to be trusted and are largely believed to be lacking in trustworthiness by employees in organizations of all types[57]. The principles of ethical stewardship offer an opportunity for leaders to redefine relationships in organizations, but those basic principles are rarely fully appreciated. The following are five guidelines, however, for leaders who seek to become ethical, principle-centered, and value-based ethical stewards.

---

[55] This point is profoundly made by Pfeffer, J., (1998), op. cit. and by Beer, M., (2009). *High Commitment, High Performance: How to Build a Resilient Organization for Sustained Advantage*. San Francisco, CA: Jossey-Bass.

[56] *Ibid.*

[57] Harrington, M., (2017), *op. cit.*

1. Leadership is about Service to Others and Treating Others with Kindness, Dignity, and Respect

Wise leaders invest in creating relationships that value people. Self-serving leaders view others as a means to their success and do not appreciate the value of others.

Leadership is a relationship. Wise leaders invest in creating relationships that **value people.** Self-serving leaders view others as **a means to their success** and **do not appreciate the value of others.**

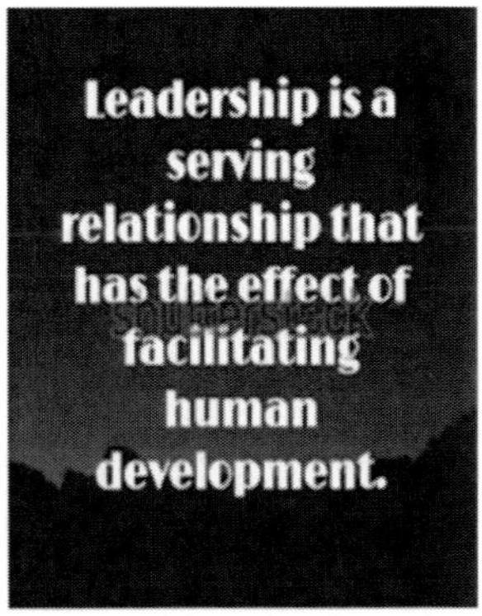

2. Effective Leaders Seek to Achieve Long-Term Value Creation Rather than Overemphasizing Short-Term Profits

Venture capitalists may seek short-term profits and a "quick killing," but leaders who are most effective recognize that they are responsible to stakeholders who depend upon a long-term relationship with the organization[58]. Focusing short-term often destroys long-term value creation[59].

---

[58] Hernandez, M., (2008), *op. cit.*
[59] Caldwell, C., Hayes, L., Karri, R., and Bernal, P., (2008), *op. cit.*

Leaders who are most effective recognize that they are **responsible to stakeholders who depend upon a long-term relationship** with the organization. **Focusing short-term** often **destroys long-term value** creation.

3. Leaders Who Are Most Respected Seek to Create Authentic Personal Relationships with Others and View Leadership as a Quasi-Sacred Obligation

Leaders must genuinely love those whom they serve[60]. Such leaders treat others as valued "Yous" and not "Its." They view the leader's obligation as a covenantal duty owed to those whom they serve[61].

Leaders must **genuinely love those whom they serve.** Such leaders treat others as valued **"Yous" and not "Its."** They view the leader's obligation as **a covenantal duty** owed to those whom they serve.

---

[60] See Anderson, V., Caldwell, C., & Barfuss, B. 2019. "Love: The Heart of Leadership." *Graziadio Business Review,* Vol. 22, Iss. 2 and may be found online at https://gbr.pepperdine.edu/2019/08/love-the-heart-of-leadership/ and Caldwell, C. and Anderson, V., (Eds.) 2019. *Leading with Love*. Hauppage, New York: NOVA Publishing.

[61] DePree, M., (2004). *Leadership is an Art*. New York: Crown Publishing.

4. Leaders Earn the Trust and Commitment of Others by Being Impeccably Ethical and Moral

Ethical obligations are implicit in the leadership role[62]. The psychological contract demands that leaders honor others and treat them with a commitment to their welfare, growth, and wholeness. Failing to fulfill that moral obligation demonstrates that leaders lack integrity[63].

The **psychological contract** demands that **leaders honor others and treat them with a commitment to their welfare, growth, and wholeness.** Failing to fulfill that **moral obligation** demonstrates that leaders lack **integrity.**

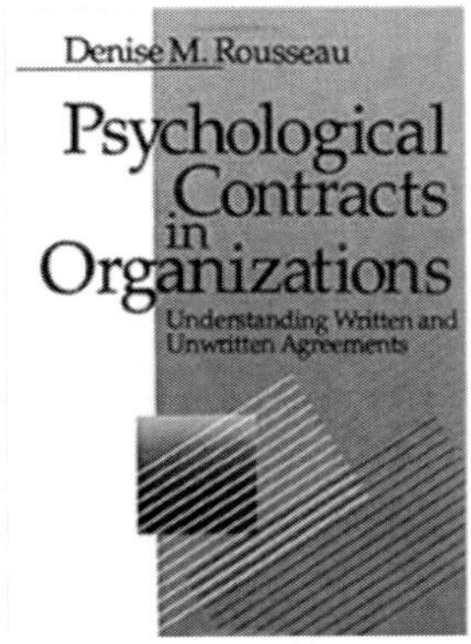

5. Leaders Hold Both Themselves and Others Accountable and Willingly Accept Personal Responsibility

Leadership is always about accountability and responsibility[64]. Leaders who fully understand their role view themselves as personally accountable when organizations make mistakes, but willingly give credit to others when their organizations succeed[65]. Although such leaders strive unceasingly to be

---

[62] Hernandez, M., (2008), *op. cit.*

[63] This ethical obligation of leaders is constantly made by scholars. See Covey, S. R., (2004), *op. cit.* and Caldwell, C., (2012). *Moral Leadership: A Transformative Model for Tomorrow's Leaders*. New York: Business Expert Press.

[64] Covey, S. R., (1992). *Principle-Centered Leadership*. New York: Fireside Press and Collins, J., (2001) and Collins, J., (2001). *Good to Great: Why Some Companies Make the Leap. . . . And Others Don't*. New York: Harper Collins.

[65] *Ibid.*

the best version of themselves, their focus is on the organization's purpose and they care deeply about it and its membership[66].

Leaders who fully understand their role **view themselves as personally accountable** when organizations make mistakes, but willingly give credit to others when their organizations succeed. Although such leaders **strive unceasingly to be the best version of themselves**, their focus is on the **organization's purpose** and they **care deeply about it and its membership.**

Applying the guidelines of ethical stewardship is no simple task – though the principles may seem to be "common sense." Those who strive to be truly great leaders constantly evaluate themselves, willingly acknowledge their shortcomings, and never cease to become the best possible version of themselves.

Those who strive to be truly great leaders **constantly evaluate themselves**, willingly **acknowledge their shortcomings**, and never cease to **become the best possible version** of themselves.

[66] DePree, M., (2004), *op. cit.*

Conclusion

Within each one of us is a person who has the potential to become a great person and an outstanding leader. That potential is God given and often beyond our ability to full imagine[67] – but it is most assuredly there. That embryo of excellence is not in some of us. . . it is in all of us, even if we have not been able to see it[68].

The inspiring example of people like S. Truett Cathy confirms that it is possible to incorporate true principles into our daily lives, as well as into our businesses. The moral obligation to become truly honorable stewards and to serve others is a source of great personal satisfaction – a satisfaction that, unfortunately, many people never discover. To those individuals who seek to become the best version of themselves, the life of S. Truett Cathy is a source of inspiration – and a testament that we have within ourselves the potential to serve others, honor God, and achieve great things.

The **moral obligation** to become **truly honorable stewards** and to **serve others** is a source of **great personal satisfaction** – a satisfaction that, unfortunately, **many people never discover**.

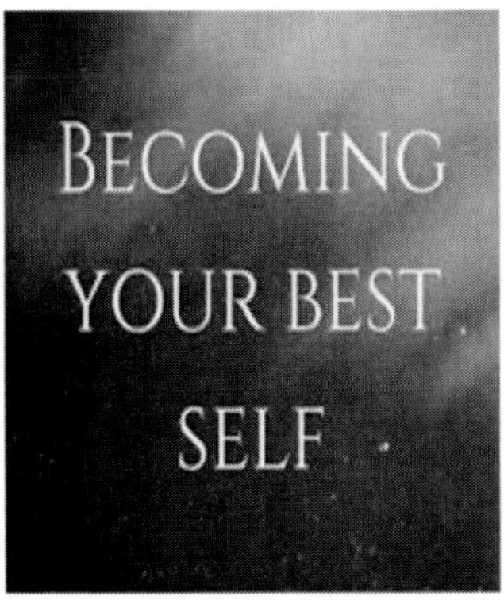

[67] Many are the individuals who have affirmed this great truth. See, for example, Williamson, M., (1996). *A Return to Love: Reflections on the Principles of "A Course in Miracles."* New York: Harper One.

[68] *Ibid.*

Chapter 3

LEADERS PREPARE FOR CHANGE: THE OMNIPRESENT REALITY

The **responsibility of every leader** is to prepare herself or himself for the **demands of constant change** that affect **each individual life**, the **organizations** in which men and women work, and **every nuance of the world around them.**

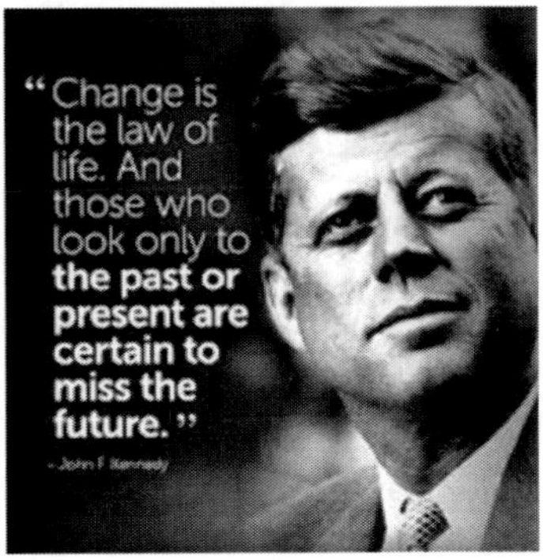

Every person and every organization must adapt to the constant forces of change. President John F. Kennedy explained that change is the law of life – and that those who failed to look to the future would be certain to miss it[69]. The responsibility of every leader is to prepare herself or himself for the demands of constant change that affect each individual life, the

[69] The precise quote is "Change is the law of life. And those who look only to the past or present are certain to miss the future." See "Leadership and Change Quotes." *AZ Quotes.* Found online on December 25, 2019 at https://www.azquotes.com/quotes/topics/leadership-and-change.html.

organizations in which men and women work, and every nuance of the world around them.

No individual and no organization can avoid the pressures of constant change and the leader's role is to personally prepare for change, to help others with whom they work to be ready, and to guide their organizations through the change process. Although the management function typically focuses on maintaining the status quo, the role of leadership recognizes that change is inevitable and must be wisely anticipated.

No individual and no organization can avoid the pressures of constant change and **the leader's role is to personally prepare for change**, to **help others** with whom they work **to be ready**, and to **guide their organizations** through the change process.

The purpose of this chapter is to identify the factors that are vital to lead individuals and organizations in the change process. After identifying those key variables, the barriers to change that leaders face are then described. The leadership role of Darwin Smith, Chief Executive Officer (CEO), in guiding the change at Kimberly-Clark is cited as an example of a leader who successfully coordinated the change process. His success is contrasted with that of the failure of the leader of a major department store CEO in its financial decline. Five important factors are identified insights for leaders to remember as they address the pressures of change. The chapter concludes with encouragement to leaders as they prepare for constant change.

LEADING CHANGE

The leader's role in ensuring that an organization is responsive to the demands of change is well established. Creating a culture that responds quickly to constant change and that pursues continuous improvement is not only a major responsibility of the modern leader but determines whether an organization can be responsive to the external environment and adaptable internally[70]. The change process is unique to virtually every organization, but the commonalities involve eight stages[71].

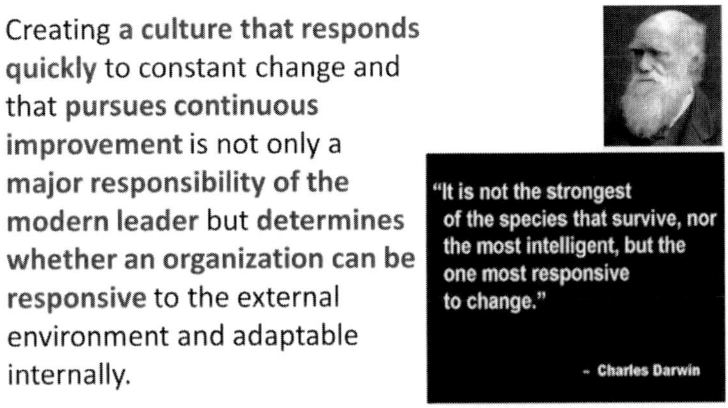

1. Create a Sense of Urgency

People are reluctant to make a change until they accept the idea that the change required is urgently needed. Once individuals believe that a change is necessary to achieve their goals, they are then ready to be active participants.

---

[70] The leader's role in creating organizational culture is the theme of Schein, E. H. & Schein, P. A., (2016). *Organizational Culture and Leadership* (5th ed.). Hoboken, NJ: Wiley.

[71] The eight stages of change are contained in the widely respected book on change by Harvard University's John Kotter. The eight stages contained herein come from Kotter, J. P., (2012). *Leading Change, With a New Preface by the Author*. Boston, MA: Harvard Business Review Press.

People are **reluctant to make a change** until they accept the idea that the **change required is urgently needed.** Once individuals **believe that a change is necessary** to achieve their goals, they are then **ready to be active participants**.

2. Form a Powerful Coalition

Key participants who are respected and recognized as important organizational leaders provide legitimacy to the change process and can be advocates and champions for change. Those supporters then increase the credibility of those who direct the change and the legitimacy of the entire change process.

Key **participants who are respected** and recognized as important **organizational leaders provide legitimacy** to the change process and **can be advocates and champions for change.** Those supporters then **increase the credibility** of those who direct the change and **the legitimacy of the entire change process.**

3. Create a Vision for Change

Identifying a clear vision for change requires explaining what the change will look like but will also provide a convincing justification for the reason for the change in terms that organization members can then accept. The vision should inspire participants and offer a better alternative than the past or the status quo.

Identifying a **clear vision for change** requires explaining **what the change will look like** but will also provide a **convincing justification** for the reason for the change in terms that organization members can then accept. The vision should **inspire participants and offer a better alternative** than the past or the status quo.

visionfor
change

4. Communicate the Vision

Communicating the vision requires explaining what it means, the steps required to achieve it, and the manner in which those steps will be carried out. That explanation should also clarify for individual organization members the roles that they will play to make the vision a reality.

Communicating the vision requires **explaining what it means**, the **steps required** to achieve it, and the manner in which **those steps will be carried out**. That explanation should also **clarify** for individual organization members **the roles** that they will play **to make the vision a reality.**

5. Remove Obstacles

Barriers to the successful achievement of any change are always likely to impair the process and need to be anticipated and effectively addressed. Resources must be available to not only remove obstructing obstacles but to make the steps to change achievable and sustainable.

Barriers to the successful achievement of any change are always **likely to impair the process** and need to be anticipated and effectively addressed. Resources **must be available** to not only **remove obstructing obstacles** but to **make the steps** to change **achievable and sustainable**.

6. Create Short-Term Wins

Leaders of the change process need to predetermine opportunities for meaningful "victories" to affirm to organization members that the change process is working and to encourage their efforts. The required resources to create those short-term wins need to be in place and delivered, as needed.

Leaders of the change process need to predetermine opportunities for **meaningful "victories" to affirm** to organization members that **the change process is working** and to **encourage** their efforts. The **required resources** to create those short-term wins **need to be in place and delivered**, as needed.

7. Build on the Change

A strategy must be in place to demonstrate steady improvement in implementing changes that are necessary. The implementation of that strategy depends upon providing the support systems and resources to reinforce the fact that the change process is making measurable headway.

A strategy must be in place to **demonstrate steady improvement** in implementing changes that are necessary. The implementation of that strategy depends upon **providing the support systems and resources** to reinforce the fact that **the change process is making measurable headway.**

8. Anchor the Change into the Culture

Change requires establishing values that help to create a new perspective and a new organizational culture. Declaring victory too soon and before that culture is in place and adopted throughout an organization makes it possible for individuals to adopt practices that are part of the former culture and that erode the change process.

Change requires **establishing values that help to create a new perspective** and a new organizational culture. **Declaring victory too soon** and before that culture is in place and adopted throughout an organization **makes it possible for individuals to adopt practices that are part of the former culture** and that erode the change process.

Anchor the Culture Change

Harvard University's John Kotter emphasized that each of these eight steps is necessary to ensure an organizational change that is sustainable and that redefines an organization[72]. The leader's challenge is to recognize the importance of each of the steps necessary to initiate a change and to see it through to a productive conclusion[73].

The **leader's challenge** is to **recognize the importance of each of the steps** necessary to initiate a change and **to see those steps through** to a **productive conclusion.**

[72] *Ibid.*

[73] Schein, E. H. & Schein, P. A., (2016), *op. cit.*

Darwin Smith's Management of Change

Although a classic example of a humble and unassuming leader[74] Darwin Smith was brilliant at managing change at the once stodgy company, Kimberly-Clark. At the time that Smith took over as Chief Executive Officer (CEO) in 1971, "the company languished in mediocrity, the bulk of its capital tied up in giant paper mills[75]." Darwin Smith made the startling decision to sell Kimberly-Clark's paper mills – despite the fact that much of its previous business was focused on paper products and Wall Street pundits had called his decision stupid[76]. Twenty-five years later, Kimberly-Clark owned Scott Paper and outperformed Procter & Gamble in six of eight product categories[77].

Darwin Smith made the startling decision to sell Kimberly-Clark's paper mills – despite the fact that much of its previous business was focused on paper products and Wall Street pundits had called his decision stupid.

Kimberly-Clark

Darwin Smith, CEO

Smith, an understated but Harvard trained law graduate, had studied the coated paper products industry and determined that Kimberly-Clark needed to move into the consumer products industry to be successful. Despite the

[74] Smith is cited as a great example of a "Level 5 Leader" who personifies the integration of humility and a fierce resolve in Collins, J., (2001). *Good to Great: Why Some Companies Make the Leap . . . And Others Don't*. New York: HarperCollins.

[75] Collins, J., (2003). "The 10 Greatest CEOs of All Time: What These Extraordinary Leaders Can Teach Today's Troubled Executives." Fortune, July 21, 2003 and found online on December 31, 2019 at https://theclci.com/wp-content/uploads/2018/03/The10GreatestCEOsOfAllTime.pdf.

[76] Collins, J., (2001), *op. cit.*, p. 18.

[77] *Ibid*. Cited on page 18 and referencing a *Forbes* article, "The Battle of the Bottoms." (1997-98).

misgivings of some critics, Smith directed his company in its new direction and "turned Kimberly-Clark into the leading paper-based consumer products company in the world[78]." Outperforming its competitors, Kimberly-Clark's stock performance was over four times better than the general market and far superior to more famous corporate icons during the twenty years that Smith led Kimberly-Clark.

Smith had told his management team that **its success needed to be based upon identifying its strengths.** He asked them **"What could Kimberly-Clark be passionate about? What could it be best at in the world? What could improve its economics?"** Despite the widespread criticism from Wall Street and so-called "experts," Darwin Smith **focused on being right, rather than being responsive to his critics' opinions.**

The ability to ask the right question is more than half the battle of finding the answer

Smith had told his management team that its success needed to be based upon identifying its strengths. He asked them "What could Kimberly-Clark be passionate about? What could it be best at in the world? What could improve its economics[79]?" Despite the widespread criticism from Wall Street and so-called "experts," \

Darwin Smith focused on being right, rather than being responsive to his critics' opinions[80]. As a leader, Smith created great rapport with both union and non-union line workers and worked in partnership with them to refocus Kimberly-Clark[81]. During his twenty-year tenure, the company grew

---

[78] *Ibid*, page 17.

[79] Collins, J., (2003), *op. cit.*

[80] *Ibid.*

[81] "Darwin Smith – Paper Industry International Hall of Fame." *YouTube* found online on December 31, 2019 at https://www.youtube.com/watch?v=XXTNtvKRKOE.

in sales from $1 billion to $7 billion annually and the Kimberly-Clark success was largely attributed to Smith's leadership[82].

AN UNSUCCESSFUL CONTRAST

In contrast with Smith, another CEO's failure was cited as so significant that it raised the question as to whether the century-old company he led would survive his ill-fated leadership. Having been the head of retail at a major U. S. corporation and former Vice President of another large retail firm, this leader's appointment as the top executive of his new company was responded to by a surge in the stock price and enthusiasm about his "transformation vision" in guiding the retail company's future. Despite the positive predictions, this leader failed in his efforts to improve the company and within two years he was fired.

Retail sales declined by 32% in the fourth quarter of his second year as CEO and he was soon replaced, leaving the company in disgrace and acknowledged as a well-intended but unsuccessful failure. Unlike Smith, this CEO failed to focus on building a corporate culture that was consistent with many of his "radical new ideas" for rebranding the company. Without that internal ownership and cultural buy-in, the company floundered. In his wake, the company laid off thousands of employees and closed more than 800 stores nationwide.

Retail sales declined by 32% in the fourth quarter of his second year as CEO and he was soon replaced, leaving the company in disgrace and acknowledged as a well-intended but unsuccessful failure.

---

[82] Collins, J., (2003), *op. cit.*

Although this leader has been remarkably successful in two previous executive positions at major corporations, his leadership style suffered from five major faults.

1. The Culture Failed to Align with Corporate Strategy

Insufficient attention was given to training employees and changing the corporate culture. The CEO had a vision but the employees lacked an understanding of that same vision and it was not effectively communicated.

Insufficient attention was given to **training employees and changing the corporate culture**. The CEO had a vision but the **employees lacked an understanding of that same vision and it was not effectively communicated.**

2. Employees Failed to Develop Ownership and Passion

The previously conservative culture of the company was slow to buy in to the new expectations. Without passion and ownership, employees lacked a sense of urgency. Rather than creating a supportive coalition, this CEO fired many of its top managers.

The previously conservative culture of the company was **slow to buy in** to the new expectations. Without passion and ownership, **employees lacked a sense of urgency. Rather than creating a supportive coalition,** this CEO fired many of its top managers.

MORE MISTAKES

3. Customers Failed to Accept the New Image of the Old Company

In the CEO's former companies, customers readily accepted an upscale corporate image but the new long-established company failed to "sell" that new image. Customers did not buy in to the new corporate vision. The company failed to address and remove that important obstacle.

Although **marketing was creative and well-intended,** it was **never pre-tested with established customers** – who **failed to buy the new image.** By **eliminating what customers valued,** the company **failed to create short-term wins.**

Mismatch with Customer Values

4. Marketing and Branding Efforts Were Made without Understanding Customer Perceptions

Although marketing was creative and well-intended, it was never pre-tested with established customers – who failed to buy the new image. By eliminating what customers valued, the company failed to create short-term wins.

5. The Effort to Turn the Organization Inside-Out Failed due to Lack of Employee Support

Moving too quickly without creating a sense of urgency and ownership, the CEO's efforts to change the organization lacked the critical understanding and commitment of its employees. The company was unable to build on change, was undermined by it, and was unable to make the changes a part of its corporate culture.

Moving too quickly without creating a sense of urgency and ownership, the CEO's efforts to change the organization lacked the critical understanding, trust, or commitment of its employees. The company was unable to build on change, was undermined by it, and was unable to make the changes a part of its corporate culture.

Despite a well-established track record and a pedigree that demonstrated both talent and experience, this unfortunate CEO failed to guide change – with the future of the company seriously impaired and major losses resulting.

Five Insights in Leading Change

In the words of W. Edwards Deming, the Father of the Total Quality Management movement, "There is no instant pudding[83]." Deming was referring to the complex problems involved in identifying the causes of errors, obtaining employee buy-in, and improving the quality of products and services[84]. His comment applies perfectly to the challenges involved in successfully leading any meaningful organizational change.

---

[83] W. Edwards Deming is acknowledged as the individual who led the revitalization of the Japanese industrial economy after World War II and who is most associated with the Total Quality Management movement. See Deming. W. E., (2000). *Out of the Crisis*. Cambridge, MA: MIT Press.

[84] *Ibid*.

Kotter's eight-step change model identifies key organizational factors that must be addressed for changes to succeed and those eight steps are widely-acknowledged as applicable to successful change. Incorporating the wisdom of both Deming and Kotter, the following are five important leadership-related insights about the change process that are sometimes not fully understood – but that exponentially improve the likelihood of a successful change.

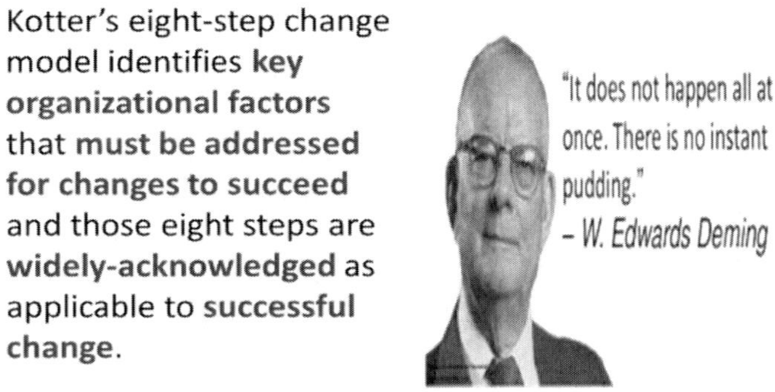

1. Change Begins with the Leader

Leaders are looked to constantly to assess their worthiness to lead and their personal credibility[85]. Only when leaders live their values are those leaders believed and willingly followed[86]. How a leader treats individual people establishes their reputation[87]. Others will not believe in the change if they do not believe in the personal integrity and character of the leader who advocates that change[88].

---

[85] Caldwell, C., and Ndalamba, K. K., (2017). "Trust and Being 'Worthy' – The Keys to Creating Wealth." *Journal of Management Development*, Vol. 36, Iss. 8, pp. 1076-1086.

[86] Schein, E. H. & Schein, P. A., (2016), *op. cit.*

[87] Covey, S. R., (1994). *The 7 Habits of Highly Effective People: Powerful Lessons in Personal Change*. Kottayam, Kerala, India: DC Books.

[88] *Ibid.*

How a leader **treats individual people** establishes **their reputation.** Others **will not believe in the change** if they **do not believe in the personal integrity and character of the leader** who advocates that change.

Leaders Build Trust by How they Treat Others

2. Every Change Requires a Rational Benefit

People must understand the rationale for the change, why the status quo is unacceptable, and the costs of maintaining the status quo**.** Providing team members with information and the reasons why change is necessary are key steps to clarifying to team members why they must change and the costs and benefits associated with change[89]. Change is so often resisted because people have a natural investment in the status quo[90]. Until people believe that there is "a better alternative," resistance to change is a natural occurrence[91].

Change is so often resisted because **people have a natural investment in the status quo.** Until people believe that there is "a better alternative," **resistance to change is a natural occurrence.**

---

[89] The resistance to change is well documented. See, for example, Kotter J.P. & Schlesinger L.A. (1989) "Choosing Strategies for Change" in D. Asch & C. Bowman (Eds.) *Readings in Strategic Management*. London: Palgrave Macmillan, pp. 294-306.

[90] *Ibid.*

[91] *Ibid.*

3. Change Succeeds When People become Owners and Partners

Involving employees at all levels and **making them full owners and partners** is also necessary for change to occur – and is **a principle that is well established as a key factor** of effective leadership.

From serving as a member of a guiding coalition to participating as individual employees in carrying out change-related tasks, personal ownership is essential in the change process[92]. Members of the guiding coalition should be carefully-chosen and should possess their own personal credibility[93]. However, involving employees at all levels and making them full owners and partners is also necessary for change to occur – and is a principle that is well established as a key factor of effective leadership[94].

4. Each Change Requires Necessary Resources

Leaders must clearly understand which resources are required for a successful change to occur – and must be able to ensure that those resources will be available[95]. A useful process for monitoring the resources required for individual tasks involves working closely with teams assigned to accomplish those important tasks[96]. Until teams have access to the necessary resources, there can be no change[97].

---

92 Kotter, J. P., (2012), *op. cit.*

93 *Ibid.*

94 The importance of treating employees as owners and partners is well established in Block, P., (2013). *Stewardship: Choosing Service Over Self-Interest*. San Francisco, CA: Jossey-Bass.

95 Kotter, J. P., (2012), *op. cit.*

96 The process for effective change and quality improvement is described in Scholtes, P. R., Joiner, B. L. & Streibel, B. J., (2018). *The TEAM Handbook* (3rd ed.). Hooksett, NH: Goal/QPC.

97 *Ibid.*

Leaders must clearly understand **which resources are required** for a successful change to occur – and must be able to **ensure that those resources will be available.**

5. Successful Change is a Cultural Phenomenon

Only when an organizational culture has changed permanently will a planned change persist[98]. A successful cultural change requires careful attention on the part of an organization's Top Management Team and the willingness of that team to hold supervisors and managers at all levels accountable for modeling the values and standards of the new culture[99]. Typically, a permanent cultural change requires many months to successfully introduce and instill. The leader's example and her/his commitment to the new cultural values are important contributors to such a change[100].

Typically, **a permanent cultural change** requires **many months** to successfully introduce and instill. The **leader's example** and her/his **commitment to the new cultural values** are important contributors to such a change.

---

[98] Kotter, J. P., (2012), *op. cit.*
[99] Schein, E. H. & Schein, P. A., (2016), *op. cit.*
[100] *Ibid.*

Incorporating these five insights, along with the steps outlined by Kotter, can make an organizational change more effective and can address the natural investment that employees have in the status quo. By carefully planning the change process and by creating the structure and supports that are required to implement a transition, leaders can make a desired change easier to implement and can enable an organization to respond to the constantly evolving world in which they compete.

CONCLUSION

The constant challenges of an ever-changing world demand that leaders understand the process of change, the difficulties to overcome, the steps required to make change successful, and the resources needed to implement those steps[101]. Inevitably, the successful leader must recognize that her/his personal example and commitment to the highest standards are the keys to being perceived as capable, credible, and competent[102].

Inevitably, the successful leader must recognize that her/his **personal example and commitment** to the **highest standards** are the keys to **being perceived as capable, credible, and competent.**

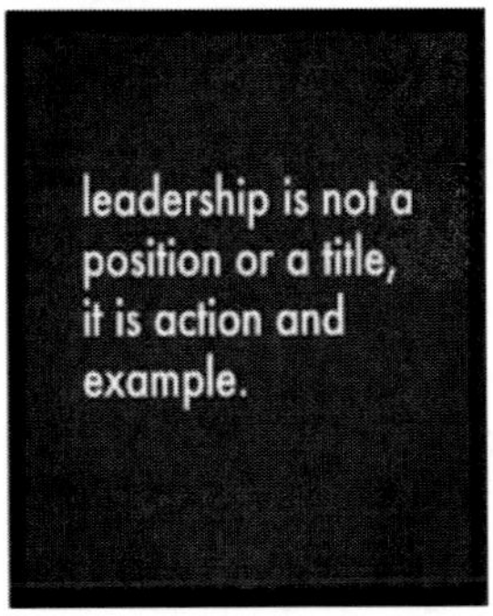

The outstanding success of Darwin Smith at Kimberly-Clark and the failure of the retail company led by a leader who did not adequately understand the nuances of change provide powerful examples of the importance of applying the principles of change that require careful

---

[101] Kotter, J. P., (2012), *op. cit.*
[102] Caldwell, C., and Ndalamba, K. K., (2017), *op. cit.*

preparation, personal commitment, and organizational resources. The latter example demonstrates that even leaders who have previously been successful in one organization can seriously misread the context in which they seek to introduce change in a new setting.

Even leaders who have previously been successful in one organization can seriously misread the context in which they seek to introduce change in a new setting.

This chapter also reinforces the critical need for leaders to understand the tremendous importance of their own values, their personal integrity, their commitment to the success of their organization, and their attitude towards those employees and individuals with whom they work and who they serve as organizational leaders. As leaders honor their responsibilities as ethical stewards committed to others and their best interests, they expand their ability to influence others, to earn their trust and commitment, and to successfully guide their organizations in a world of constant change.

As leaders honor their **responsibilities as ethical stewards** committed to others and their best interests, they **expand their ability to influence others, to earn their trust** and commitment, and to **successfully guide** their organizations **in a world of constant change.**

Chapter 4

INTEGRITY AND ITS CONSEQUENCES: THE FOUNDATION OF LEADERSHIP

Despite its importance for leaders and organizations, **integrity is perceived to be in short supply** in organizations of all types and recent research confirms that **leaders struggle to be perceived as credible and trustworthy.**

The research about leadership makes it abundantly clear that a leader's integrity is overwhelmingly considered to be the quality most valued by both a leader's peers and her/his followers[103]. Integrity is at the foundation of trustworthiness and is the standard of conduct expected of honorable men

[103] Kouzes, J. M. & Posner, B. Z., (2011). *Credibility: How Leaders Gain and Lose It, Why People Demand It*. San Francisco, CA: Jossey-Bass.

and women[104]. Despite its importance for leaders and organizations, integrity is perceived to be in short supply and recent research confirms that leaders struggle to be perceived as trustworthy[105].

The focus of this chapter is on explaining the significance of integrity as a leadership quality and to present two contrasting examples of leaders. One leader has been known for his great integrity and the lack of personal integrity of the other leader resulted in his personal disgrace, the loss of millions of investor dollars, and the individual ultimately being sent to jail for financial fraud. The chapter begins by defining identity, based upon the insights of several scholars. It then identifies five important characteristics of integrity and contrasts those characteristics with the qualities of individuals who lack integrity.

The chapter then chronicles the powerful example of Jon Huntsman, Sr. -- a leader known for living a life of great integrity. Huntsman's **integrity is then contrasted with the lack of integrity** of another individual who, though brilliant in many ways, failed to honor his obligations as Chief Executive Officer of one of the largest and most highly regarded companies in the United States.

The chapter then chronicles the powerful example of Jon Huntsman, Sr. – a leader known for living a life of great integrity. Huntsman's integrity is then contrasted with the lack of integrity of another individual who, though brilliant in many ways, failed to honor his obligations as Chief Executive Officer of one of the most highly regarded companies in the United States.

---

[104] Mayer, R. C., Davis, J. H. & Schoorman, F. D., (1995). "An Integrative Model of Organizational Trust." *Academy of Management Review*, Vol. 20, No. 3, pp. 709-734.

[105] Clifton, J. & Harter, J., (2019). *It's the Manager: Gallup Finds the Quality of Managers and Team Leaders is the Single Biggest Factor in Your Organization's Long-term Success.* Omaha, NE: Gallup Press.

The chapter concludes by offering five insights about the nature of integrity and the obligations that it imposes to guide leaders who may seek to honor the responsibilities associated with being a person of integrity.

Integrity has been described as **the "most commonly cited morally desirable trait"** and the **foundation of successful relationships.**

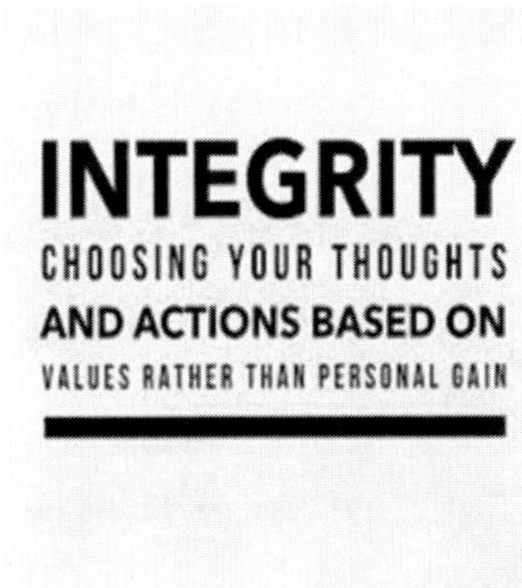

The Importance of Integrity

Integrity has etymological roots in the French ***integrité***, meaning blamelessness and purity, and in the Latin ***integritatem***, which meant wholeness, completeness, or correctness[106]. Integrity has been described as the "most commonly cited morally desirable trait[107]" and the foundation of successful relationships. Integrity has been defined in a variety of ways by scholars and wordsmiths. The following are six of the many ways in which integrity is described:

- Harvard's Eugene Soltes described integrity as the appropriate behavior established by "the norms set by its leaders.[108]" Divergence

---

[106] See "integrity" retrieved from the *Online Etymology Dictionary,* found online on December 10, 2019 at https://www.etymonline.com/word/integrity.

[107] Audi, R. & Murphy, P. E., (2006). *Business Ethics Quarterly*, Vol. 16, Iss. 1, pp. 3-21.

[108] This phrasing is found on page 51 of Soltes, E., (20109). "Where is Your Company Most Prone to Lapses in Integrity?" *Harvard Business Review*, Vol. 97, Iss. 4, pp. 51-54.

from integrity results in "misconduct" that can harm the firm and its reputation – in addition to creating regulatory and liability risks[109].

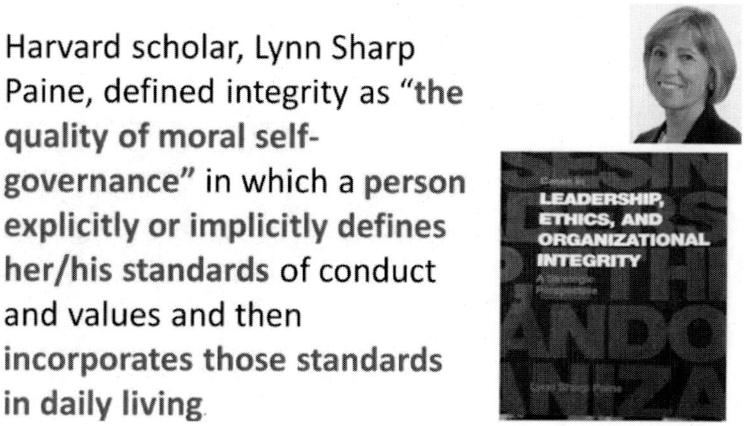

- Another Harvard scholar, Lynn Sharp Paine, defined integrity as "the quality of moral self-governance[110]" in which a person explicitly or implicitly defines her/his standards of conduct and values and then incorporates those standards in daily living.
- Richard De George of the University of Kansas defined integrity as acting according to one's highest self-accepted standards of behavior and imposing on oneself the duties demanded by the highest ethical and moral criteria[111].
- Cox and his colleagues defined integrity as the imperfect but best effort to be in control of one's actions – suggesting that "integrity is about managing self-conflict well" and that integrity involves taking the self to be constantly in an inconsistent and evolving state[112].

---

[109] *Ibid.*

[110] Paine, L. S., (1997). "Integrity." In *The Blackwell Encyclopedic Dictionary of Business Ethics*, Werhane, P H. and Freeman, R. E. (eds.). Oxford: Blackwell Publishers, Ltd. 335-336.

[111] De George, R. (1993). *Competing with Integrity in International Business*. New York: Oxford University Press

[112] Cox, D., La Caze, M. & Levine, M. P. (2003). *Integrity and the Fragile Self*. New York: Routledge.

Integrity as the **imperfect but best effort to be in control** of one's actions and "is about **managing self-conflict well**" and taking the self to be **constantly in an inconsistent and evolving state.**

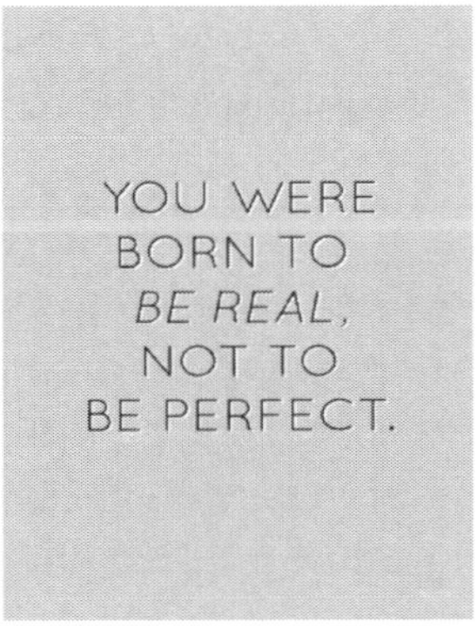

- Yang and colleagues define integrity as consistency between a person's words and actions and equate integrity with the best elements of "spiritual leadership[113]." These scholars define integrity and spiritual leadership in terms of the vision and value congruence of those who lead – as opposed to the leadership of those who adopt a religiously-based leadership persona[114].
- According to Audi and Murphy, integrity is a moral virtue and a composite of multiple factors[115].
    1. *Conscience* – An innate sense of right and wrong driven by an inner feeling or voice
    2. *Will* – The self-discipline and internal capacity to control one's actions and respond appropriately.
    3. *Beneficence* – Interpersonal behaviors demonstrating genuine caring and consideration of others.
    4. *Value Loyalty* – Commitment to the personal values that one has adopted, despite the costs.
    5. *Principles* – A belief in a specific set of ethical and moral standards that have universal relevance.

---

[113] Yang, F., Liu, J., Wang, Z. & Zhang, Y., (2019). "Feeling Energized: A Multilevel Model of Spiritual Leadership, Leader Integrity, Relational Energy, and Job Performance." Journal of Business Ethics. Vol. 158, Iss. 4, pp. 983-997.

[114] *Ibid.*

[115] Audi, R. & Murphy, P. E., (2006), *op. cit.*

6. *Application* – Incorporation of a practical implementation plan for translating beliefs into daily action.

Each of these six related definitions associated with integrity affirms the importance of an individual embracing a set of ethical standards for her/his own conduct – typically requiring the self-discipline required to carry out behaviors consistent with those standards in establishing relationships with others and in being true to oneself.

Each of these six related definitions associated with integrity affirms the importance of an individual embracing a set of ethical standards for her/his own conduct – typically requiring the self-discipline to carry out behaviors consistent with those standards in establishing relationships with others and in being true to oneself.

Unfortunately, as Princeton's David Callahan has noted, we live in a world that he characterized as "the cheating culture" in which leaders and individuals at all organizational levels who possess integrity are often notable and even considered unique[116]. Despite the decline in moral values and the lack of trustworthiness and integrity by which many would-be leaders are viewed, there are nonetheless remarkable leaders who possess great integrity and are valued highly by both their followers and their peers[117].

---

[116] Callahan, D., (2004). *The Cheating Culture: Why More Americans Are Doing Wrong to Get Ahead*. New York: Mariner Books.

[117] Kouzes, J. M. & Posner, B. Z., (2011), *op. cit.*

Despite the decline in moral values and the lack of trustworthiness and integrity by which many would-be leaders are viewed, there are nonetheless remarkable leaders who possess great integrity and are valued highly by both their followers and their peers.

Dr. Maya Angelou
Multi-talented

Nelson Mandela
Political Leader

Sanna Marin
Prime Minister of Finland

Five Key Characteristics of Integrity

Leadership integrity is directly related to the ways in which that quality affects the identity or inner nature of each individual. For a person to possess integrity, that individual's life reflects qualities that are typically lacking in many other individuals. The following are five key characteristics that distinguish an individual as a man or woman of integrity.

1. Integrity Is the Fruit of a Healthy Personal Identity and Positive Self-Esteem

People with integrity view themselves in as positive light and seek to become the best version of themselves[118]. A leader with integrity strives to

---

[118] Stephen R. Covey calls this ability to become our best version of ourselves "finding our voice." See Covey, S. R., (2004). *The 8th Habit: From Effectiveness to Greatness*. New York: Free Press.

fulfill her/his own potential, to speak the truth, and to honor self and others. Such leaders understand that dishonesty, even if undiscovered, erodes their inner peace, impairs self-esteem, and undermines the leader's confidence in relationships[119].

A leader with integrity strives to fulfill her/his own potential, to speak the truth, and to **honor self and others**. Such leaders understand that **dishonesty, even if undiscovered, erodes their inner peace, impairs self-esteem, and undermines the leader's confidence** in relationships.

2. Integrity Requires High Personal Regard for Others and a Sense of Responsibility to Them

People with integrity greatly value the worth of others and acknowledge and honor their duties and moral responsibilities owed to others. Such leaders view themselves as ethical stewards – viewing their role as creating long-term value for society and serving others – rather than simply pursuing their own personal gain and self-interests[120].

---

[119] This quote from the author, Cheryl Hughes. See "Integrity Quotes." *Goodreads* found online on December 9, 2019 at https://www.goodreads.com/quotes/tag/integrity.

[120] This concept is addressed in many sources. See, for example, Hernandez, M., (2008). "Promoting Stewardship Behavior in Organizations: A Leadership Model." *Journal of Business Ethics*, Vol. 80, Iss. 1, pp. 121-128, and Caldwell, C., Bischoff, S. J., and Karri, R. (2002). "The Four Umpires: A Paradigm for Ethical Leadership," *Journal of Business Ethics*, Vol. 36, Iss. 1/2, pp. 153-163.

Integrity has nothing to fear, no duplicity, and nothing to hide. There is no intention to deceive, to manipulate, or to take advantage of others. No attempt is made to misrepresent personal beliefs or to hide behind a façade.

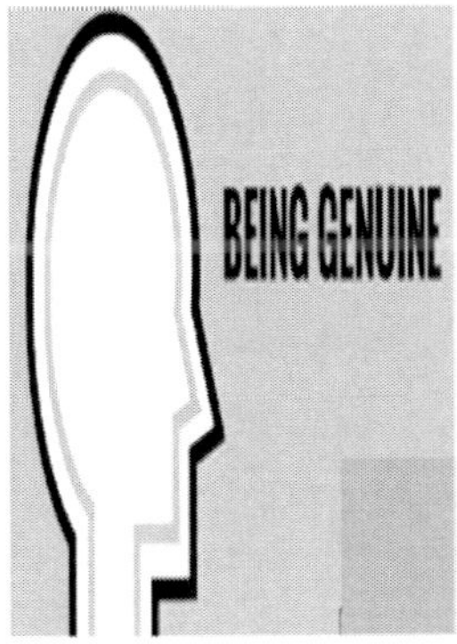

3. With Integrity There Is No Pretense or Misrepresentation of Oneself

Individuals with integrity are comfortable with who they are. Integrity has nothing to fear, no duplicity, and nothing to hide[121]. There is no intention to deceive, to manipulate, or to take advantage of others. No attempt is made to misrepresent personal beliefs or to hide behind a façade.

Honesty consists of "more than not lying. It is truth telling, truth speaking, truth living, and truth loving."

James E. Faust

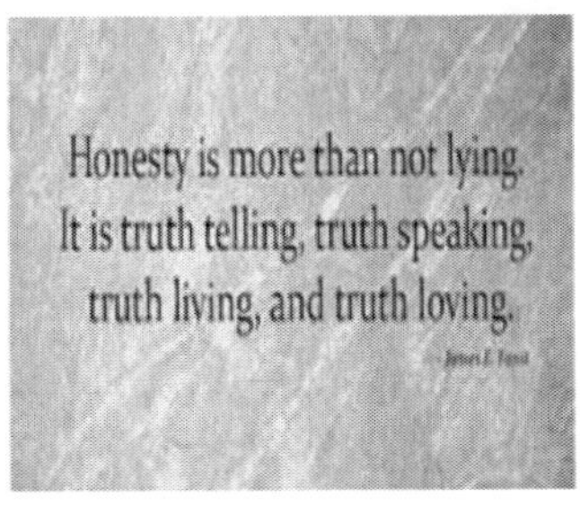

[121] See, for example, a quote by Zig Ziglar. See Mead, A. (N.D.). "30 Inspirational Quotes on Integrity." *Awaken the Greatness Within*. Found online on December 10, 2019 at https://www.awakenthegreatnesswithin.com/30-inspirational-quotes-on-integrity/.

4. Integrity Is Alignment Between What a Person Says and What (S)He Actually Does

A person with integrity knows who (s)he is and conveys what (s)he stands for by her/his words and with accompanying actions[122]. In the words of James E. Faust, honesty and integrity consist of "more than not lying. It is truth telling, truth speaking, truth living, and truth loving[123]."

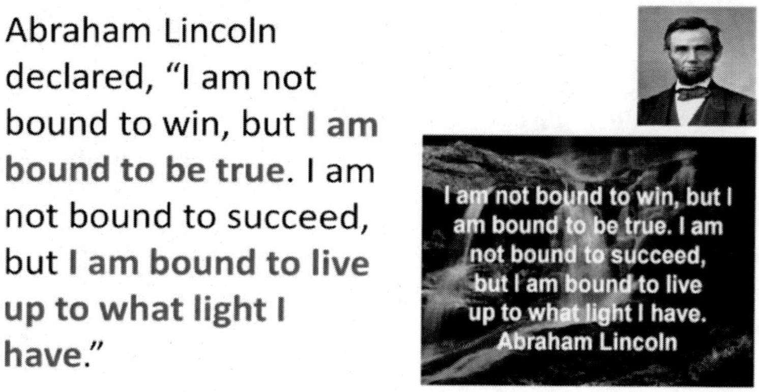

5. Integrity Does Not Require Perfection but Demands Both Humility and Commitment

Individuals with integrity do not claim to be perfect, acknowledge their shortcomings, yet are constantly striving to improve. They relate to the words of Abraham Lincoln who declared, "I am not bound to win, but I am bound to be true. I am not bound to succeed, but I am bound to live up to what light I have[124]."

---

[122] This insight comes from New York Times best selling author, Spencer Johnson. *Ibid.*
[123] James E. Faust, the highly regarded religious leader, offered these words. *Ibid.*
[124] This Abraham Lincoln quote is famous. *Ibid.*

As Atticus Finch declared in Harper Lee's ***To Kill a Mockingbird***, "(B)efore I can live with other folks, **I have to live with myself**. The one thing that does not abide by majority rule is a person's conscience." **Men and women of integrity steadfastly follow their conscience** – and by so doing they demonstrate **the noble quality of Spiritual Intelligence.**

Leaders with integrity refuse to settle for mediocrity but strive to constantly improve – never giving up, despite temporary set-backs or personal failures[125]. As Atticus Finch declared in Harper Lee's *To Kill a Mockingbird,* "(B)efore I can live with other folks, I have to live with myself. The one thing that does not abide by majority rule is a person's conscience[126]." Men and women of integrity steadfastly follow their conscience – and by so doing they demonstrate the noble quality of Spiritual Intelligence[127]. Integrity is "not a conditional word. It does not blow in the wind or change with the weather[128]."

Einstein reminded us that leaders lacking integrity in small matters are typically "careless with the truth" and "cannot be trusted with important matters[129]." Those who lack integrity cut corners, convey only the parts of the truth that they want others to know, and use information and their own persona and shadow to manipulate others and to deceive[130]. The cost of

---

[125] Hughes, C., *op. cit.*

[126] The words are from Lee's protagonist, Atticus Finch. See Lee, H., (2005). *To Kill a Mockingbird*. New York: Harper Perennial.

[127] Stephen R. Covey equates the conscience with Spiritual Intelligence in his book, *The 8th Habit*. See Covey, S. R., (2004), *op. cit.*

[128] John D. MacDonald was an American writer of novels and short stories.

[129] This Albert Einstein quote is found at "Integrity Quotes." *Goodreads* found online on December 9, 2019 at https://www.goodreads.com/quotes/tag/integrity, *op. cit.*

[130] This point is made clearly in the work of Carl Jung and his discussion of the persona and the shadow in the human personality. See Jung, C. G., (2006). *The Undiscovered Self: The Dilemma of the Individual in Modern Society*. New York: Signet and Caldwell, C., (2000). *Communication, Meaning, and Identity: Moving Toward Discovery*. Hauppage, NY: NOVA Publishing.

dishonesty and a lack of integrity is that others ultimately recognize a dishonest leader's intentions and hypocrisy. Failing to live what one professes destroys trust and is the antithesis of integrity.

The cost of dishonesty and a lack of integrity is that others ultimately recognize a dishonest leader's intentions and hypocrisy. Failing to live what one professes destroys trust and is the antithesis of integrity.

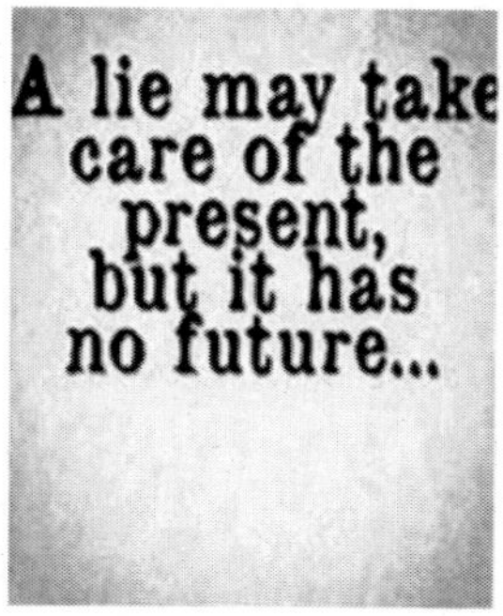

JON HUNTSMAN, SR. AND INTEGRITY

Jon Huntsman, Sr. lived a life that was legendary and exemplified the classic American dream. Huntsman was born to humble circumstances but rose to become a business leader, a widely-respected church man, and a generous philanthropist to numerous significant causes[131]. Jon Huntsman, Sr. lived a life consistent with the high personal values that he espoused and he was known widely for his uncompromising personal integrity.

Huntsman founded and was executive chairman of Huntsman Corporation, a global manufacturer and marketer of specialty chemicals[132]. Huntsman strongly opposed the idea that ethical principles varied from country to country and the story of the development of his business worldwide reinforced his reputation for unwavering personal integrity and good business sense[133].

---

[131] Huntsman's amazing achievements are chronicled in many places. See, for example, his autobiography. Huntsman, J., Sr., (2014). *Barefoot to Billionaire: Reflections on a Life's Work and a Promise to Cure Cancer*. New York: Harry N. Abrams Publishers.

[132] *Ibid.*

[133] *Ibid.*

Jon Huntsman, Sr. strongly **opposed the idea that ethical principles varied** from country to country and the story of the development of his business worldwide reinforced his reputation for unwavering personal integrity and good business sense. Huntsman's **reputation for service to others and dedication to correct principles** characterized his entire life.

Jon Huntsman, Sr.

Huntsman's reputation for service to others and dedication to correct principles characterized his entire life. As a philanthropist, he founded libraries and buildings at several universities – as well as the Huntsman Cancer Institute (HCI). The motto of the HCI typified his own values, and Huntsman once said "For me, the true measure of success is not how much wealth you acquire but how much of it you give back[134]." Huntsman's philosophy of life and his commitment to correct principles are reflected in his highly-regarded book, *Winners Never Cheat: Even in Difficult Times*[135]. To Jon Huntsman, Sr., he truly believed that his purpose in life was to serve others, to honor God, and to become the best version of himself[136].

At Huntsman's passing at the age of 80, his contributions to the world were cited by many prominent admirers. Called, "one of the greatest Utahns to ever live" by Utah Governor, Gary Herbert, Huntsman was a man beloved by thousands for his devotion to correct principles, his love of others, and his personal example[137]. Though one of Utah's "lions," Huntsman was

---

[134] Huntsman's personal mantra is found in several places. This quote is found from the Forbes list of billionaires. The profile on Jon Huntsman Sr. found on December 9, 2019 at https://www.forbes.com/profile/jon-huntsman-sr/#61f3aa0f10b4.

[135] Huntsman, J. M. Sr., (2008). *Winners Never Cheat: Even in Difficult Times, New and Expanded Version*. Hoboken, NJ: Pearson FT Press.

[136] *Ibid.*

[137] Johnson, B., (2018). "Jon Huntsman, Sr. Passes Away." *BlockU.com*, February 2, 2018 and found online on December 8, 2019 at https://www.blocku.com/2018/2/2/16966998/jon-huntsman-sr-passes-away.

beloved for his personal example and generosity in many parts of the world[138].

The Lack of Integrity

Although a Harvard trained MBA known for his brilliant intelligence, the individual who demonstrated a major deficit in integrity was the Chief Executive Officer and former Chief Financial Officer of one of America's most highly respected firms. Financial and accounting manipulations, securities and wire fraud, and the conspiracy to defraud are among the list of the 19 counts for which this individual was found guilty.

Claiming ignorance of the financial manipulations that ultimately **destroyed his firm and cost investors billions** of dollars, this individual was nonetheless **found guilty of a multitude of felonies and ultimately became the poster child for top executive hubris, wholesale dishonesty, and personal self-seeking.**

Claiming ignorance of the financial manipulations that ultimately destroyed his firm and cost investors billions of dollars, this individual was nonetheless found guilty of a multitude of felonies and ultimately became the poster child for top executive hubris, wholesale dishonesty, and personal self-seeking. Ordered to pay a $180 million fine and to repay the government

---

[138] Wharton School, (2018). "Remembering Jon M. Huntsman, Sr.: Lessons from a Compassionate Leader." University of Pennsylvania February 6, 2018 and found online on December 9, 2018 at https://knowledge.wharton.upenn.edu/article/remembering-jon-m-huntsman-sr-lessons-compassionate-leader/.

$630 million in total, this individual served twelve years in federal prison – but his actions impacted thousands of investors, ruined their lives, and cost many their financial security.

As troubling as his personal dishonesty and his lack of integrity is **his desire, since being recently released from jail, to now reenter the business world** and to engage **in the same industry in which he robbed many of their financial security.**

The value of the shares of the firm he led dropped from a healthy $90 per share to 26 cents, virtually overnight, as the truth about this leader's financial dishonesty became public knowledge. His firm went from being one of America's "Wall Street darlings" to being virtually bankrupt overnight. As troubling as his personal dishonesty and his lack of integrity is his desire, since being recently released from jail, to now reenter the business world and to engage in the same industry in which he robbed many of their financial security.

INSIGHTS FOR LEADERS

Because integrity is such a vital requirement for leaders who wish to be trusted by others – and because achieving others' trust is so vital for interpersonal and organizational success – current or would-be leaders would be wise to refine their understanding of the nature of integrity and its requirements for leaders. The following are five important insights for individuals who seek to be perceived as a person of integrity.

Because integrity is such **a vital requirement for leaders who wish to be trusted by others** – and because **achieving others' trust is so vital** for interpersonal and organizational success – **current or would-be leaders would be wise to refine their understanding of the nature of integrity** and its requirements for leaders.

1. Integrity Begins with a Healthy Identity and High Personal Self-Regard

At the root of successful interpersonal relations is the ability to perceive oneself as a person of value[139]. By attaining this positive self-assessment, an individual is then capable of holding herself or himself accountable to standards which make up her or his identity and to begin to be accountable to oneself and to others[140].

At the root of successful interpersonal relations is the ability to **perceive oneself as a person of value.** By attaining this positive self-assessment, **an individual is then capable of holding herself or himself accountable to standards which make up her or his identity** and to begin to be accountable to oneself and to others.

Self-Regard and valuing oneself require being accountable to high standards.

[139] Erich Fromm describes this self-regard as the ability of a person to love herself or himself. Lacking this ability, an individual is unable to establish healthy relationships with others. See Fromm, E., (2006). *The Art of Loving*. New York: Harper Perennial.

[140] The nature of the identity standard, described in detail by Peter Burke and Jan Stets, explains the process by which individuals hold themselves personally accountable. See Burke, P. J. & Stets, J. E., (2009). *Identity Theory*. Oxford, UK: Oxford University Press.

2. Integrity Requires a Regard for Others and an Appreciation of Their Value

As individuals develop a healthy self-regard, they are then able to begin to appreciate others and to recognize their value[141]. That recognition motivates individuals to strive to learn, to grow, and to improve in order to serve others better – and to establish standards for themselves as they create relationships with other people[142].

As individuals develop a healthy self-regard, they are then **able to begin to appreciate others and to recognize their value.** That recognition **motivates individuals to strive to learn, to grow, and to improve in order to serve others better – and to establish standards for themselves** as they create relationships with other people.

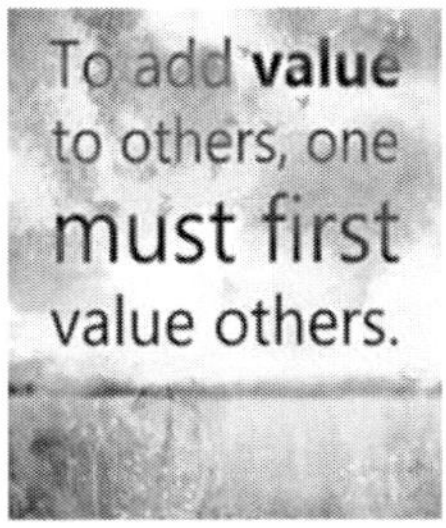

3. Integrity Is Founded upon a Belief in Universal Principles of Fairness and Morality

Ethical conduct and moral behavior are based upon the assumption that there are correct principles that govern relationships between people and within organizations[143]. Those universal principles become the foundation for a healthy society and for effective organizations[144]. Integrity is ultimately about ethical and moral conduct and is the foundation of ethical leadership[145].

---

[141] Fromm, E., (2006), *op. cit.*

[142] This point is well established by many scholars. See, for example, Caldwell, C. and Anderson, V., (Eds.) 2019. *Leading with Love*. Hauppage, New York: NOVA Publishing.

[143] This concept is well established. See, for example, Solomon, R. C., (1992). *Ethics and Excellence: Cooperation and Integrity in Business*. New York: Oxford University Press.

[144] For insights about the importance of universal principles, see Lewis, C. S. & Norris, K., (2015). *Mere Christianity*. New York: Harper One and Covey, S. R., (1992). *Principle-Centered Leadership*. New York: Fireside Press.

[145] Caldwell, C., (2012). *Moral Leadership: A Transformative Model for Tomorrow's Leaders*. New York: Business Expert Press.

Ethical conduct and moral behavior are **based upon the assumption that there are correct principles that govern relationships** between people and within organizations. Those universal principles become **the foundation for a healthy society and for effective organizations.**

4. Integrity Includes the Ability to Hold Oneself Accountable to One's Personal Ethical Standards

Believing in correct principles and understanding their importance is not enough[146]. Integrity requires the ability to match one's beliefs and values with one's personal conduct and is the willingness to be personally accountable for actions that align with one's personal beliefs[147].

Integrity requires the ability to **match one's beliefs and values with one's personal conduct** and is the willingness to **be personally accountable** for actions that align with one's personal beliefs.

[146] This critical point is made by Schein, E. H. & Schein, P. M., (2016). *Organizational Culture and Leadership* (5th ed.). San Francisco, CA: Jossey-Bass.

[147] Covey, S. R., (2004), *op. cit.*

5. Integrity Does Not Require Perfection in Behavior but It Does Include a Commitment to Continuous Improvement in the Pursuit of One's Ideals

Leaders do not need to be perfect to be perceived as trustworthy[148]. However, they must be persons of character who are committed to be accountable for their actions, to acknowledge that accountability, and to be willing to change their actions and make good their intentions[149]. By demonstrating their commitment to right conduct, leaders honor their commitments and maintain a reputation for integrity – even if and when they stumble and make mistakes.[150]

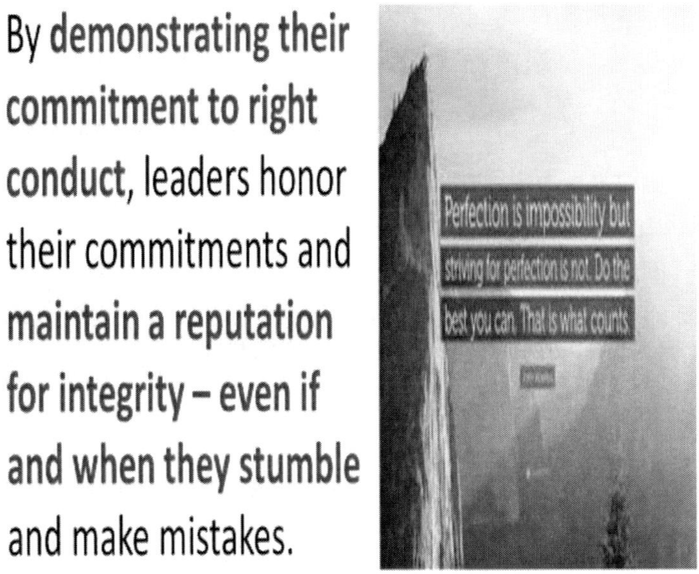

---

[148] *Ibid.*

[149] Covey, S. R., (1992), *op. cit.*

[150] This important point is made in Kouzes, J. M. & Posner, B. Z., (2017). *The Leadership Challenge: How to Make Extraordinary Things Happen in Organizations* (6th ed.). San Francisco, CA: Jossey-Bass.

These five insights can be a powerful resource in enabling individuals who wish to emulate integrity to govern themselves and their actions. Integrity is a profoundly high standard of performance – but its value in earning the trust and commitment of others is essential for establishing great relationships and for creating successful organizations.

CONCLUSION

Great leaders are the exception in the modern organization. Generating profits is not enough – although profits are, of course, absolutely necessary for businesses to succeed. However, leaders can be more successful than their peers if they add integrity to their arsenal when interacting with others – both within their organization and with customers and other stakeholders[151].

Leaders can be **more successful than their peers if they add integrity** to their arsenal when interacting with others -- both **within their organization and with customers and other stakeholders.**

The positive example of Jon Huntsman, Sr. and the actions of his negative counterpart provide powerful testimony to the importance of leaders demonstrating integrity. Huntsman's overwhelming success occurred not just because he had integrity but because he combined that integrity with other necessary skills to achieve personal and professional

---

[151] This point is extraordinarily clear and emphasized over and over again by scholars who study successful organizations. See, for example, Pfeffer, J., (1998). *The Human Equation: Building Profits by Putting People First*. San Francisco, CA: Jossey-Bass.

goals that have benefited thousands. In contrast, the negative example cited herein is an example of a brilliant individual who lost his way and compromised his integrity – destroying not only his own reputation but robbing thousands of others of their savings.

As individuals of all types seek to become people of integrity, the ability to apply the fundamental truths upon which integrity is based will enable those people to not only improve their organizations and enhance their relationships but become happier and healthier individuals themselves.

Trust, the commitment of others to follow a leader and to cooperate in the pursuit of shared goals, is vital to creating great organizations[152]. As important, trust is also the key to all interpersonal relationships and is the most important factor for developing connection and uniting people for their mutual benefit. As individuals of all types seek to become people of integrity, the ability to apply the fundamental truths upon which integrity is based will enable those people to not only improve their organizations and enhance their relationships but become happier and healthier individuals themselves.

---

[152] The importance of trust in organizations is well documented. See, for example, Covey, S. R., (2004), *op. cit.*, and Caldwell, C. and Anderson, V., (Eds.). (2019). *Trust, Trustworthiness, and Stewardship: A Transformative Approach*. Hauppage, New York: NOVA Publishing.

Chapter 5

HONORING OTHERS: KINDNESS, TRUST, AND LEADERSHIP

Leaders who are kind honor others are ethical and moral in working for others' success and demonstrate key qualities of trustworthiness[153]. In his outstanding book, *Leadership is an Art*, Max DePree explained that organization leaders have a "covenantal" duty to honor others[154].—requiring leaders to recognize that their obligation included being a true "servant and a debtor" who recognized that greatness in organizations was achieved when leaders demonstrated a sacred commitment to individual employees and their welfare[155].

---

[153], C., (2017). "Kindness and Self-Interest: Why Treating Employees Well Makes Such Good Sense." *Graziadio Business Review*. Vol 20, Iss. 1, found online at http://gbr.pepperdine.edu/2017/04/kindness-and-self-interest/. This citation emphasizes that kindness is a critical condition precedent for establishing the trustworthiness of a leader.

[154] See DePree, M., (2004). Leadership is an Art. New York: Crown Publishing, p. 11-15.

[155] *Ibid.*

In his outstanding book, ***Leadership is an Art***, Max DePree explained that organization leaders have a "covenantal" duty to honor others. That role, DePree wrote, required leaders to recognize that their obligation included being a true "servant and a debtor" who recognized that greatness in organizations was achieved when leaders demonstrated a sacred commitment to individual employees and their welfare.

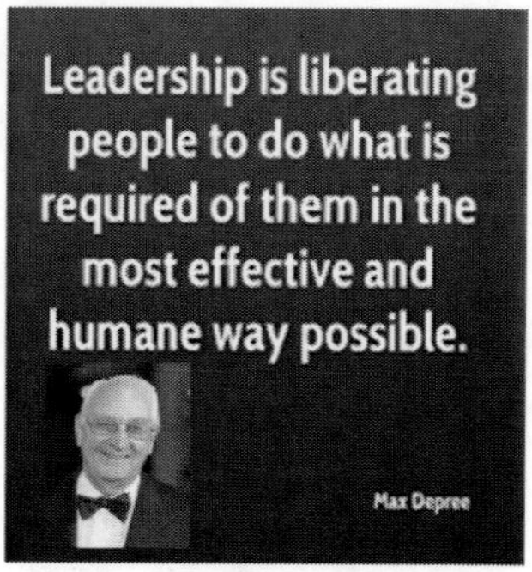

Leadership, according to Stephen R. Covey, means treating others so well that they come to recognize their greatness and strive to achieve it[156]. When employees become the best version of themselves, their organizations benefit as well[157]. By being kind to others and demonstrating a genuine commitment to others' welfare, leaders go a long way in earning the trust of others.

The focus of this chapter is on explaining the nature of kindness as a leadership quality that transcends simply treating others with dignity and respect – although that element of kindness is also important. In today's world of arms-length employer-employee relationships, leaders who are kind set the tone for their entire organization and, by so doing, they create an organizational culture that breeds high trust and commitment.

After explaining the nature of kindness and its opposite as leadership qualities, this chapter identifies two examples of leaders – one who epitomized kindness as a moral virtue and another who seemed to lack the qualities of kindness. By describing these two leaders, the chapter contrasts the impact of the leaders' behaviors on the organizations where these leaders served. After documenting six key contributions about kindness and its related elements, the chapter then concludes with four recommendations for individuals who seek to be recognized as kind and trustworthy leaders.

---

[156] This definition of leadership identifies the leader's moral obligation to helping others to achieve greatness. See page 98 of Covey, S. R., (2004). *The 8th Habit: From Effectiveness to Greatness*. New York: Free Press.

[157] *Ibid*, p. 99.

In today's world of arms-length employer-employee relationships, **leaders who are kind set the tone for their entire organization** and, by so doing, they **create an organizational culture that breeds high trust and commitment.**

UNDERSTANDING KINDNESS

Kindness has been described as "a complex transformational behavior that demonstrates that one person understands and cares genuinely about another's welfare, growth, and wholeness[158]," Harold Kushner, the prominent Jewish Rabbi, suggested that we do things for others, not because of who they are but because of who we are[159]. Kindness, then, becomes a byproduct of our identity, how we see the world, and the perceived duties that we believe we owe to others. Kindness is both an expression of Aristotelian virtue ethics and a reflection of our moral identity which conveys to others the integration of both the cognitive or rational and the affective or emotional[160].

Harold Kushner, the prominent Jewish Rabbi, suggested that we do things for others, **not because of who they are but because of who we are.** Kindness, then, becomes **a byproduct of our identity, how we see the world, and the perceived duties** that we believe we owe to others.

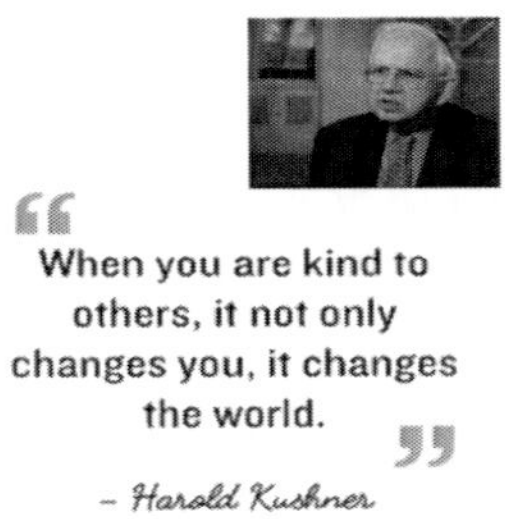

[158] Caldwell, C., (2017), *op. cit.*

[159] "Harold S. Kushner Quotes." *Goodreads* found online on November 20, 2019 at https://www.goodreads.com/author/quotes/26180.Harold_S_Kushner.

[160] DeTienne, K. B., Ellertson, C. F., Ingerson, M-C. & Dudley, W. R., (2019). "Moral Development in Business Ethics: An Examination and Critique." *Journal of Business Ethics.*

As a key requirement for leaders to be perceived as trustworthy, kindness is widely recognized as an antecedent to trust[161]. Kindness includes both the benevolent intention to demonstrate a commitment to another person and accompanying beneficent action that reflects that intention[162]. When demonstrated by leaders toward employees and colleagues, kindness can become a source of competitive advantage – differentiating trustworthy leaders and organizations from those that give lip service to treating employees as valued assets but fail to match that verbiage with their actions[163].

When demonstrated by leaders toward employees and colleagues, kindness can become **a source of competitive advantage – differentiating trustworthy** leaders and organizations **from those that give lip service** to treating employees as valued assets but **fail to match that verbiage with their actions.**

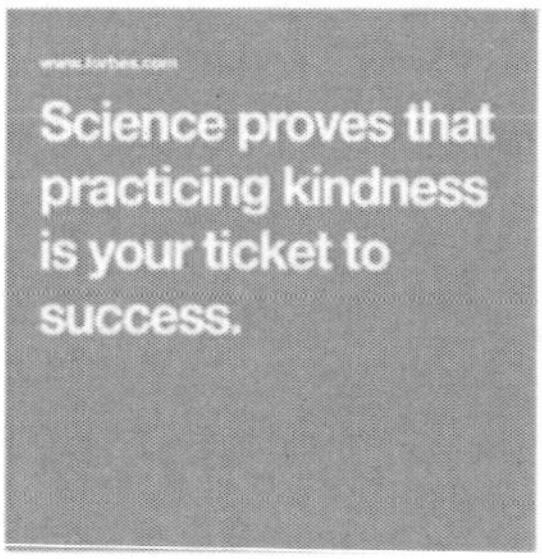

Implicit in kindness is the obligation to do more than to simply empathize, or to put oneself in another's position. Kindness, or beneficence, is an action that translates empathy into compassionate service[164]. By demonstrating that they genuinely care about those with whom they work, leaders earn others' confidence and commitment – thereby benefiting the

---

[161] A frequently cited article about trust and trustworthiness is Mayer, R. C., Davis, J. H. & Schoorman, F. D., (1995). "An Integrative Model of Organizational Trust." *Academy of Management Review*, Vol. 20, No. 3, pp. 709-734.

[162] Caldwell, C., Floyd, L. A., Taylor, J and Woodard, B. (2014). "Beneficence as a Source of Competitive Advantage." *Journal of Management Development*, Vol. 33, Iss. 10, pp. 1057-1069.

[163] *Ibid.*

[164] Caldwell, C., Atwijuka, S., & Okpala, C. O. "Compassionate Leadership in an Arms-Length World." Working draft.

individual served while raising the level of trust within the entire organization[165]. Because of the positive organizational and interpersonal benefits of treating others as valued partners, rather than as commodities, leading with kindness is replete with moral obligations as well as positive outcomes[166].

> Because of the positive **organizational and interpersonal benefits** of **treating others as valued partners**, rather than as commodities, **leading with kindness is replete with moral obligations** as well as positive outcomes.

BEING UNKIND AND ITS CONSEQUENCES

At the interpersonal level, people who are unkind are looked upon by others as lacking in basic goodness. Kindness is viewed as a virtue, and behavior that is lacking that basic element immediately generates a negative response from others[167]. Failing to demonstrate basic interpersonal sensitivity to others is perceived as both a character flaw and a deficit in emotional and spiritual intelligence[168].

---

[165] This important point is made is Schein, E. H. & Schein, P. A., (2016). *Organizational Culture and Leadership* (5th ed.). San Francisco, CA: Jossey-Bass.

[166] Caldwell, C., (2017), *op. cit.*

[167] Cameron, K. (2011). "Responsible Leadership as Virtuous Leadership." *Journal of Business Ethics*, Vol. 98, pp. 25-35.

[168] Covey, S. R., (2004), *op. cit.*

Kindness is viewed as a virtue, and behavior that is **lacking that basic element** immediately generates a **negative response** from others. **Failing to demonstrate basic interpersonal sensitivity** to others is perceived as **both a character flaw and a deficit in emotional and spiritual intelligence.**

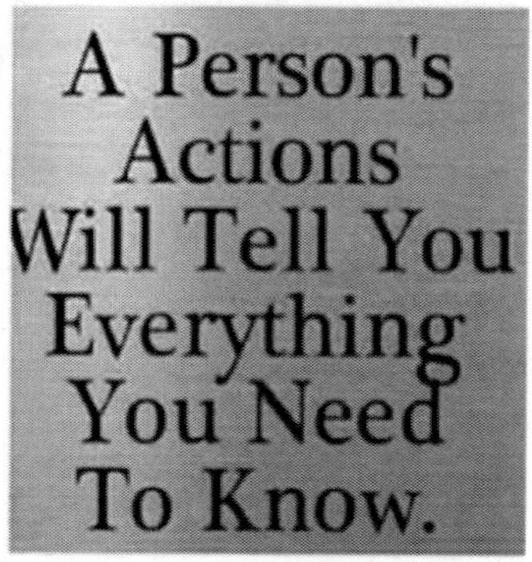

Being unkind is immediately manifest when an individual is dishonest with others – particularly when that behavior is also self-serving and detrimental to others' welfare. Self-serving behaviors tend to give priority to achieving a short-term outcome – but when unkind and dishonest behaviors are discovered by others, the impact of such conduct is to destroy organizational trust and erode relationships and the reputations of those who are dishonest. Thus, dishonest, self-serving, short-term "benefits" are actually detrimental to the long-term best interests of a leader and undermine the commitment and effectiveness of the entire organization[169].

When **unkind and dishonest behaviors** are discovered by others, the impact of such conduct is to **destroy organizational trust and erode relationships** and the reputations of those who are dishonest.

[169] Gates, D., (2017). "Self-Interest, Ethics, and Success." BYU Wheatley Institution, September 26, 2017 and found online on November 30, 2019 at https://wheatley.byu.edu/self-interest-ethics-and-success/.

Because kind and compassionate actions are so essential to a leader's reputation and such a clear indication of Emotional Intelligence, unkind and insensitive conduct is also notable by its contrast with moral leadership communicates to others that a leader is not only insensitive but unwise. Rather than honoring the moral standard of ethical stewardship and the "covenantal" relationship of great leaders, unkind leaders treat others like "means" to their own short-term interests rather than as "ends" to whom they owe sacred obligations[170].

Rather than honoring the moral standard of **ethical stewardship and the "covenantal" relationship** of great leaders, unkind leaders treat others like **"means"** to **their own short-term interests rather than as "ends"** to whom they owe sacred obligations.

Leaders establish the values of their organization by their examples and by the implicit standards that they demonstrate to others.[171] The leader's example is the single most important factor that determines an organization culture and the standards by which others interact within an organization[172]. For that reason, the legal doctrine of *respondeat superior* holds the leader responsible for the actions of her or his employees—acknowledging the leader's role in defining the standards by which key members of the organization treat other employees as they emulate the leader's example[173].

---

[170] The distinction between these two disparate philosophies has been identified by dozens of authors. See, for example, Hernandez, M., (2008). "Promoting Stewardship Behavior in Organizations: A Leadership Model." *Journal of Business Ethics*, Vol. 80, Iss. 1, pp. 121-128.

[171] Schein, E. H. & Schein, P. A., (2016), *op. cit.*

[172] Ibid.

[173] See "Respondeat Superior Law and Legal Definition" *US Legal.com* found online on November 30, 2019 at https://definitions.uslegal.com/r/respondeat-superior-doctrine/.

The legal doctrine of ***respondeat superior*** **holds the leader responsible** for the actions of her or his employees—**acknowledging the leader's role in defining the standards** by which key members of the organization treat other employees as they emulate the leader's example.

Respondeat Superior

Liability for the wrong committed by others.

As with other examples of personal conduct, one's degree of kindness is reflected on a virtuous continuum[174]. The diagram of a virtuous continuum provided below demonstrates the range of behaviors associated with personal conduct that a person may choose.

Virtuous	Moral	Amoral	Immoral
Seeks to optimize long-term value creation and magnifies duties owed to all stakeholders.	Adds value, keeps commitments to stakeholders and society, and obeys laws.	Avoids breaking the law but may act with short-term self-interest rather than that of others.	Seeks outcomes that maximize perceived self-interest and avoid self-harm.

Ironically, personal behavior that treats others unkindly may be perceived as in one's short-term self-interest, but Covey has noted that such behavior is noted by others – and when a leader is unkind and self-serving (s)he ultimately harms her/his own reputation as third parties observe that

[174] This virtuous continuum has been addressed by many scholars and builds on the work of Kim Cameron, David Whetten, and Archie Carroll who have all identified the continuum of virtuous conduct. See, for example, Caldwell, C., Hasan, Z., and Smith, S. (2015). "Virtuous Leadership: Insights for the 21st Century." *Journal of Management Development*. Vol. 34, Iss. 9, pp. 1181-1200 and Caldwell, C., Carter, E., and Floyd, L. A., (2015). "Coaching for Improved Teaching: A Virtuous Model for Improving Performance and Increasing Commitment." *Business and Management Research*, Vol. 4, No. 4, pp. 54-65.

conduct[175]. Thus, treating others kindly is both a moral and ethical responsibility and a behavior that is increasingly being recognized as in a leader's self-interest[176].

Stephen R. Covey has noted that when a leader is unkind and self-serving (s)he ultimately harms her/his own reputation as third parties observe that conduct. Thus, treating others kindly is both a moral and ethical responsibility and a behavior that is increasingly being recognized as in a leader's self-interest.

As noted by many scholars, the dysfunction of leaders and organizations is a common occurrence – often reflecting the neuroses and unethical conduct of leaders who fail to understand their moral obligations and the importance of treating others with kindness, respect, and regard[177]. The examples of Malden Mills' Chief Executive Officer, Aaron Feuerstein and those actions of a University President in the Western United States are profoundly contrasting examples of kind and unkind leadership behaviors in demonstrating the degree to which leaders honor others or dishonor themselves by their example and interactions.

As noted by many scholars, the dysfunction of leaders and organizations is a common occurrence – often reflecting the neuroses and unethical conduct of leaders who fail to understand their moral obligations and the importance of treating others with kindness, respect, and regard.

---

[175] Stephen R. Covey has identified the profound importance of leaders treating each person in a virtuous manner and the impact of that treatment – as observed by others – on a leader's reputation. See Covey, S. R., (1992). *Principle-Centered Leadership*. New York: Fireside Press.

[176] Caldwell, C., (2017), *op. cit.*

[177] See, for example, Kets de Vries, M. F. R. & Miller, D., (1991). *The Neurotic Organization: Diagnosing and Revitalizing Unhealthy Companies* (2nd ed.). New York: HarperCollins.

KINDNESS AND AARON FEUERSTEIN

In 1995, a catastrophic fire in Lawrence, Massachusetts destroyed Malden Mills, the complex of the community's largest employer[178]. The fire was the largest in Massachusetts history and eliminated employment for 3,000 of the company's employees just before Christmas[179]. Aaron Feuerstein, the company's Chief Executive Officer and third-generation owner of the family business, could have walked away with a $300 million insurance settlement. Instead, Feuerstein gathered his employees and told them that for the next sixty days they would all receive full salaries – and Feuerstein also committed to rebuilding the Malden Mills plant[180].

Aaron Feuerstein, the company's Chief Executive Officer, and third-generation owner of the family business, **could have walked away with a $300 million insurance settlement.** Instead, Feurstein gathered his employees and told them that **for the next sixty days they would all receive full salaries – and committed to rebuilding** the Malden Mills plant.

In total, Feuerstein not only rebuilt the plant in Lawrence but paid out $25 million in employee salaries, despite the fact that those employees had no work to perform and no factory in which to labor. Feuerstein eventually spent the entire $300 million insurance settlement and borrowed an additional $100 million to build both an environmentally friendly and worker friendly new plant.

Feuerstein's unprecedented acts of kindness earned not only the respect and commitment of his employees but made him a nation-wide example of

---

178 Moreno, K., (2003). "Trial by Fire." Forbes, April 14, 2003 and found online on December 6, 2019 at https://www.forbes.com/forbes/2003/0414/092.html#3fa8ec4b6391.

179 Leung, R., (2003). "The Mensch of Malden Mills." *CBS News 60 Minutes*, July 2003 and found online on December 6, 2019 at https://www.cbsnews.com/news/the-mensch.

180 *Ibid.*

an employer who demonstrated that which he personally believed[181]. Citing the Jewish Torah, Feuerstein played down his decision – insisting that what he was doing was simply his obligation to the working man and to the Lawrence community[182].

Aaron Feuerstein's decision has been repeatedly cited as the epitome of moral and ethical conduct that best symbolizes an employer's virtuous obligation to others. By treating his employees as valued partners and as people to whom he owed a sacred duty, Feuerstein demonstrated a level of kindness that literally shocked not only the business community but academics, politicians, and the news media[183].

Feuerstein's **unprecedented acts of kindness** earned not only the **respect and commitment** of his employees but made him a **nation-wide example** of an employer who **demonstrated that which he personally believed.**

As an example of the kindness of a leader to those being led, Aaron Feuerstein honored his personal commitment to others. His kindness regarding others' and their welfare is as highly regarded as any other leadership action in recent history. Feuerstein treated others with a full appreciation of the "covenantal" standard of duty to which the best leaders are accountable[184]. Unfortunately, Feuerstein's acts of kindness seem to be the rare exception, rather than the rule, in today's arms-length employer-employee work environment where employees are more likely to be treated as commodities rather than as people[185].

---

[181] *Ibid.*
[182] *Ibid.*
[183] *Ibid.*
[184] DePree, M., (2004), *op. cit.*
[185] See, for example, Pfeffer, J., (1998). *The Human Equation: Building Profits by Putting People First.* Boston, MA: Harvard Business Review Press.

Unfortunately, Feuerstein's acts of kindness seem to be the rare exception, rather than the rule, in today's arms-length employer-employee work environment where **employees are more likely to be treated as commodities rather than as people.**

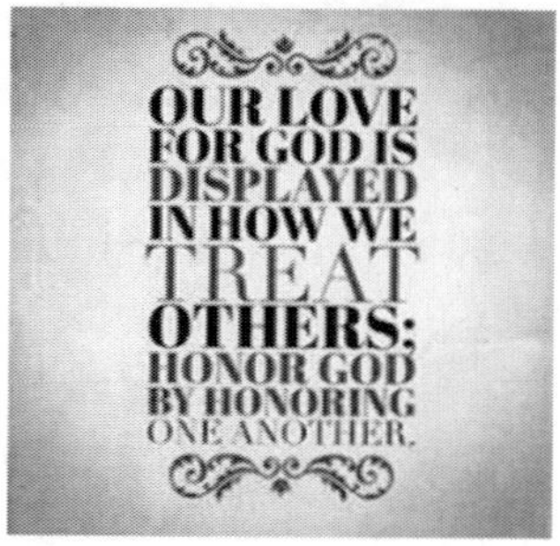

Failure to Be Kind

The antithesis of Feuerstein's kindness is found in the recent actions of a university president in a small Western United States community that has seen its university grow in size due largely to extensive advertising and an open enrollment policy. Unfortunately, the agenda of the president seems to be on maintaining and increasing student enrollment and obtaining Division 1 athletic status rather than improving the quality of academic instruction. Although the university has enjoyed rapid growth, it has struggled for more than a decade with student retention, with the quality of its academic offerings, and with the employability of its graduates.

The **antithesis of Feurstein's kindness** is found in **the recent actions of a university president** in a small Western United States community that has seen its university grow in size due largely to **extensive advertising and an open enrollment policy.** Unfortunately, the agenda of the president seems to be on maintaining and **increasing student enrollment and obtaining Division 1 athletic status rather than improving the quality of academic instruction.**

Despite what can best be described as "the university's mediocre academic record," the university president and his academic vice president/provost have made academic improvement and the assessment of learning a low priority. In fact, between 2015 and 2019 the assessment of academic progress was reorganized five times – with the director of assessment no longer reporting to the academic vice president and being virtually isolated and ignored from a budgetary resource standpoint. According to the university's director of assessment – a Hispanic woman – upon asking for additional resources in order to measure academic outcomes, she was told by the academic vice president that "assessment is not a priority" among his top goals.

According to the university's Director of Assessment – a Hispanic woman – **upon asking for additional resources in order to measure student academic outcomes,** she was told by the academic vice president that **"assessment is not a priority"** among his top goals.

Assessing quality of education is not a priority?

At a university?

A newly appointed administrator over institutional effectiveness once again reorganized the academic progress of the students at the university – telling the director of assessment that her position had been eliminated. In truth, no formal job analysis was conducted by the university's Human Resource Department – and a virtually identical position was established with a new title for the position.

A newly appointed administrator over institutional effectiveness **once again reorganized** the academic progress of students at the university – telling the Director of Assessment that **her position had been eliminated.**

Your Job Is

The highly qualified director of assessment, who had fourteen years of experience and a PhD in academic analysis and assessment, had been subject to years of inappropriate micro-aggressive conduct which had been reported to her supervisors but never acted upon. Despite appealing her dismissal, being told by the human resource director that it was "not a termination," and documenting her mistreatment to the university president, the director of assessment's appeal for reclassification to the university president fell upon deaf ears.

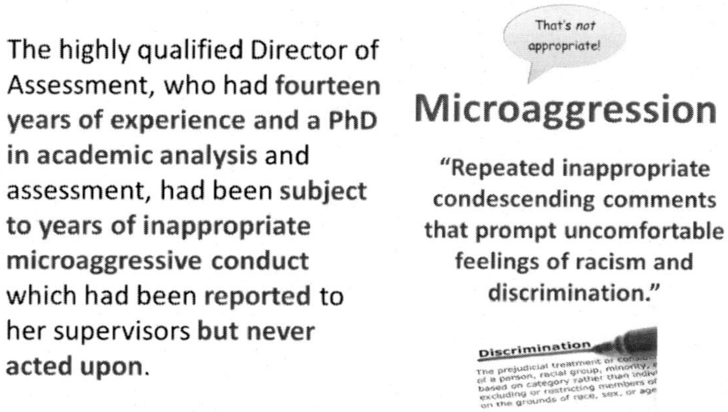

As the chief administrator of the university, this university president's actions or inactions typify the insensitivity and lack of personal consideration that occurs in many modern organizations. Like other leaders in leadership positions, the university president at this school is not only responsible for creating an organizational culture based upon treating employees with dignity and respect but is accountable for their dishonesties, administrative incompetence, and failure to act that unfortunately creates the toxic environment existing in so many modern organizations[186].

[186] For a description of the importance of the organizational leader's responsibility for creating an organizational culture and acting to ensure that its supervisors honor organizational espoused values, see Schein, E. H. & Schein, P. A., (2016), *op. cit.*.

Like other leaders in leadership positions, the university president at this school is not only **responsible for creating an organizational culture based upon treating employees with dignity and respect** but is **accountable for their dishonesties, administrative incompetence, and failure to act** that unfortunately creates the **toxic environment existing in so many modern organizations.**

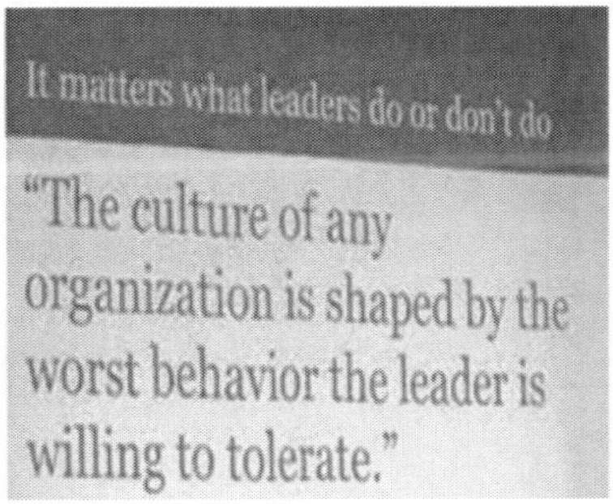

ORGANIZATIONAL IMPACTS OF KINDNESS AND ITS OPPOSITE

The sharp contrast between Aaron Feuerstein's great respect for his employees and the callous lack of empathy and common courtesy of this university president is, unfortunately, far too frequently found in today's organization--and too representative of the perspectives of many organizational leaders. The consequence of this dearth in human kindness is manifest by a multitude of surveys that affirm that 71% of employees are actively looking for new jobs, trust in leaders virtually everywhere has declined, and only 15% of employees worldwide describe themselves as positively engaged at work[187].

---

[187] Each of these findings is readily documented and each is cited in Caldwell, C. & Karri, R., (201)9. "Leadership Morality: A Transformative Philosophy Approach." the *Journal of Business and Management,* Vol. 1, Iss. 2 and available online at https:// jreslitpublications.com/business-administration-and-management/press.php,

The sharp **contrast between Aaron Feuerstein's great respect** for his employees and **the callous lack of empathy and common courtesy of this university president** is, unfortunately, **far too frequently found** in today's organizations and too **representative of the perspectives of many organizational leaders.**

The evidence from scholarly research about organizations and the importance of the values incorporated by organizational leaders is well-established. Most recently, an extensive study by Gallup has unequivocally declared, "It's the Manager[188]." Top level organizational leaders have the obligation to not only select and guide managers and supervisors but to ensure that they create organizational cultures that honor virtuous values – rather than simply posting noble but insincere platitudes on the walls of their organizations[189].

Ironically, the empirical evidence has **confirmed the common sense reality** that treating employees well can result in **increased profitability, better customer service, improved quality, and greater creativity and innovation.**

[188] The fact that managers, supervisors, and leaders are the key to organization success or failure – based upon employee responses – is the key message of the recent extensive study of Gallup. See Clifton, J. & Harter, J., (2019). *It's the Manager: Gallup Finds the Quality of Managers and Team Leaders is the Single Biggest Factor in Your Organization's Long-term Success*. Omaha, NE: Gallup Press.

[189] Schein, E. H. & Schein, P. A., (2016), *op. cit.*

Ironically, the empirical evidence has confirmed the common sense reality that treating employees well can result in increased profitability, better customer service, improved quality, and greater creativity and innovation[190]. Creating organizations with aligned human resource management policies that honor employees, treat them with high trust, and empower employees – rather than minimizing their contributions – have been demonstrated to be critical to the establishment of high trust and the implementation of high-performance work systems[191].

Such systems depend upon the honesty, integrity, competence, and kindness of organizational leaders – and the integrity and kindness of human resource professionals are also vital in conveying an organization's values[192]. As noted in the examples cited, Aaron Feuerstein created an organization that demonstrated kindness; the organization created by the university president clearly did not.

CONTRIBUTIONS OF THE CHAPTER

Kindness is not only a valued interpersonal virtue but it also has important organizational implications in building commitment, trust, and loyalty – organizational characteristics that are critical to organization success but seem to be in short supply in many organizations[193]. Because an organization mirrors the values, example, and cultural expectations of its leaders, the necessity of leaders modeling the way and holding others

---

[190] This research has been documented many times. See, for example, Pfeffer, J., (1998), *op. cit.* and Beer, M., (2009). *High Commitment, High Performance: How to Build a Resilient Organization for Sustained Advantage*.

[191] Caldwell, C., and Floyd, L. A., (2014). "High Performance Work Systems: Building Commitment to Increase Profitability." *Graziadio Business Review*, Vol. 17, Iss. 3, found online at http://gbr.pepperdine.edu/2014/12/high-performance-work-systems/.

[192] Caldwell, C., 2017. "Understanding Kindness: A Moral Duty of Human Resource Leaders." *Journal of Values-Based Leadership,* Vol. X, Iss. 2 and available online at http://scholar.valpo.edu/cgi/viewcontent.cgi?article=1188&context=jvbl.

[193] Clifton, J. & Harter, J., (2019), *op. cit.*

accountable to treating others with kindness is a virtual imperative for creating high trust[194].

Because **an organization mirrors the values**, example, and cultural expectations of its leaders, **the necessity of leaders modeling the way and holding others accountable to treating others with kindness is a virtual imperative** for creating high trust.

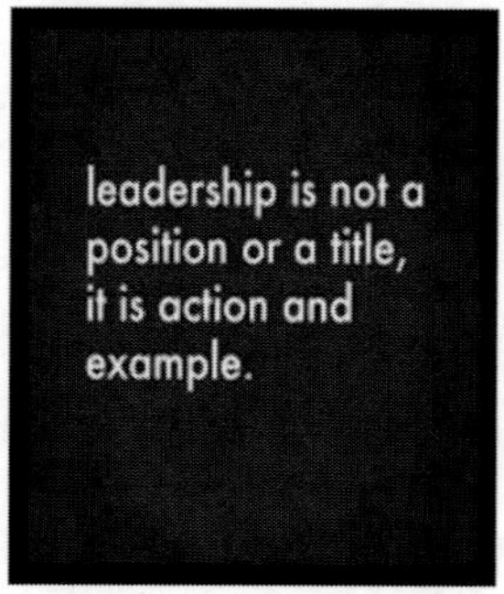

The following are six contributions made by this chapter regarding the importance of kindness, its role in organizations, and the leader's role in creating an organizational culture that models this virtue.

1. Being Unkind, as Demonstrated by Treating Employees as Commodities Rather as Partners, Erodes Employee Trust in Leaders in the Short-Term and Employee Commitment and Loyalty in the Long Term

The ultimate measure of organizations is their ability to accomplish their organizational purpose. Successful results are exponentially enhanced when leaders model the values of kindness and respect, with the evidence clearly suggesting that so many leaders, managers, and supervisors fail to recognize the value of this simple verity[195].

---

[194] Kouzes, J. M. & Posner, B. Z., (2017). *The Leadership Challenge: How to Make Extraordinary Things Happen in Organizations* (6th ed.). San Francisco, CA: Jossey-Bass.

[195] DePree, M., (2004), *op. cit*. and Covey, S. R., (1992), *op. cit*.

Successful results are exponentially enhanced **when leaders model the values of kindness and respect**, with the evidence clearly suggesting that so **many leaders, managers, and supervisors fail to recognize** the value of this simple verity.

2. The Measure of a Leader's Effectiveness Is Reflected in the Organizational Culture that (S)he Creates

When leaders demonstrate that they are committed to honoring organizational values that they espouse, they create organizational cultures where trust is high and where employee commitment grows[196]. Leaders that model the way generate the employee responses that are critical to organization success[197].

When leaders demonstrate that they are committed to **honoring organizational values** that they espouse, they **create organizational cultures where trust is high** and where employee commitment grows.

[196] Pfeffer, J., (1998), *op. cit.* and Beer, M., (2009), *op. cit.*
[197] Kouzes, J. M. & Posner, B. Z., (2017), *op. cit.*

3. Empirical Evidence Confirms that High-Trust or High-Performance Work Systems that Treat Employees with High Regard Have Proven to Be More Profitable Than Comparable Systems That Lack That Commitment to the Importance of Employees

The evidence about **organizations that align their human resource management systems,** that empower and develop employees, that **trust and invest in employees as owners and partners** of the organization, and that **deal with employees with integrity and honesty** confirms that these High-Performance Work Systems are worth the investment.

The evidence about organizations that align their human resource management systems, that empower and develop employees, that trust and invest in employees as owners and partners of the organization, and that deal with employees with integrity and honesty confirms that these High-Performance Work Systems are worth the investment[198].

4. Kindness Requires Treating Others with Dignity, Respect, Courtesy, and Compassion and Includes Being Honest

Kindness is a moral virtue in addition to a demonstration of a leader's caring about others' feelings, needs, and emotions[199]. Compassion transcends

---

[198] Beer, M., (2009), *op. cit.* and Caldwell, C. & Floyd, L. A., (2014), *op. cit.*

[199] For a review of the importance of integrity as well as kindness and caring, see Fromm, E., (2006), *The Art of Loving*. New York: Harper Perennial, DePree, M. (2004), *op. cit.*, Covey, S. R., (1992), *op. cit.*

mere empathy and demonstrates that kindness is an action – rather than simply an emotional response[200]. The leader's kindness is measured by her or his behaviors[201].

Compassion transcends mere empathy and demonstrates **that kindness is an action** – rather than simply an emotional response. **The leader's kindness is measured** by her or his behaviors.

5. Kindness Alone Is Not Enough – and Other Key Leadership Factors Must also Be Part of Successful Leadership

A leader is perceived as being trustworthy when (s)he demonstrates a combination of critical leadership skills. Kindness, caring, compassion, benevolence, and beneficence are related concepts – and, when accompanied by competence, character, the capacity to perform, and conscience – can profoundly impact a leader's ability to be perceived as trustworthy[202].

---

[200] See Caldwell, C., Atwijuka, S., & Okpala, C. O. (2018). "Compassionate Leadership in an Arms-Length World." *Journal of Business and Management* and Caldwell, C., Floyd, L. A., Taylor, J and Woodard, B. (2014). "Beneficence as a Source of Competitive Advantage." *Journal of Management Development*, Vol. 33, Iss. 10, pp. 1057-1069.

[201] Ibid.

[202] See Mayer, R. C., Davis, J. H. & Schoorman, F. D., (1995), *op. cit.* and Caldwell, C., and Ndalamba, K. K., (2017(. "Trust and Being 'Worthy' – The Keys to Creating Wealth." *Journal of Management Development*, Vol. 36, Iss. 8, pp. 1076-1086.

Kindness, caring, compassion, benevolence, and beneficence are **related concepts** – and, **when accompanied by competence, character, the capacity to perform, and conscience** – can profoundly impact a **leader's ability to be perceived as trustworthy.**

6. The Success of Current Arms-Length Employee Relationships Should Ultimately Be Measured by Long-Term Organizational Results – But Indicators of Those Long-Term Results Are Discouraging

The unfortunate reality is that today's organizations and their leaders have adopted a short-term approach to achieving organizational results[203] – an approach that treats employees like commodities rather than as valued partners[204]. This approach misrepresents the true impact of leadership accomplishments and fails to achieve the obligations of ethical stewardship which leaders owe to those whom they serve[205]. Ethical stewardship demands that leaders demonstrate a commitment to the welfare, growth, and wholeness of their employees – or acting with authentic and genuine kindness[206].

---

[203] Pfeffer, J., (1998), *op. cit.*

[204] DePree, M., (2004), *op. cit.* and Covey, S. R. (2004), *op. cit.*

[205] Cameron, K., (2011), *op. cit.* and Caldwell, C., Hayes, L., and Long, D., (2010). "Leadership, Trustworthiness, and Ethical Stewardship." *Journal of Business Ethics*, Vol. 96, Iss. 4, pp. 497-512.

[206] Caldwell, C., (2017), *op. cit.* and Caldwell, C., (2012). *Moral Leadership: A Transformative Model for Tomorrow's Leaders*. New York: Business Expert Press.

The unfortunate reality is that today's organizations and their leaders have **adopted a short-term approach** to achieving organizational results -- an approach that **treats employees like commodities** rather than as valued partners.

These six contributions reinforce the fundamental premise that leaders owe a profound moral and ethical obligation to those with whom they work in organizations – and that kindness is part and parcel of that obligation. As confirmed by Clifton and Harter in their profoundly important study about the keys to success in tomorrow's organizations, leaders and their relationships with employees ultimately determine the level of commitment, trust, and loyalty of those with whom they work[207]. It is by engaging employees and demonstrating authentic kindness and the commitment to employees' interests that leaders earn that trust[208].

Leaders and their relationships with employees ultimately **determine the level of commitment, trust, and loyalty** of those with whom they work. It is **by engaging employees and demonstrating authentic kindness and the commitment** to employees' interests that **leaders earn that trust.**

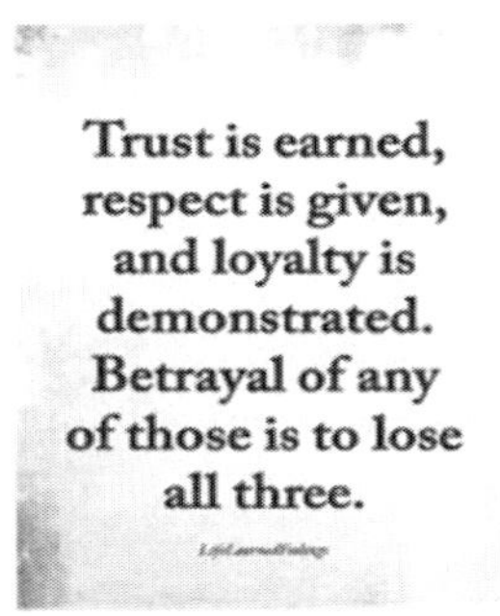

---

[207] Clifton, J. & Harter, J., (2019), *op. cit.*
[208] Caldwell, C., (2017), op. cit.

Conclusion and Recommendations

Kindness is important . . . and is "necessary" but far from sufficient for an organization to succeed and for leaders to be respected and trusted. Earning trust can be achieved by demonstrating authentic caring, genuine commitment to employees' best interests, and a passionate dedication to the purposes and goals of an organization[209]. Associated with kindness, leaders acquire that trustworthiness in four important ways.

Earning trust can be achieved by **demonstrating authentic caring, genuine commitment to employees' best interests, and a passionate dedication** to the purposes and goals of an organization.

1. Kindness Requires Valuing Others as "Yous" and Not "Its"

Great leaders understand the difference between looking at others as commodities and viewing them as full partners in the organizational relationship[210].

---

[209] The importance of these critical leadership qualities is articulated in Collins, J., (2001). *Good to Great: Why Some Companies Make the Leap . . . And Others Don't*. New York: HarperCollins, Caldwell, C., Dixon, R. D., Floyd, L., Chaudoin, J., Post, J., and Cheokas, G. (2012). "Transformative Leadership: Achieving Unparalleled Excellence." *Journal of Business Ethics*, Vol 109, Iss. 2, pp. 175-187, and Caldwell, C., (2012), *op. cit.*

[210] Treating others as valued "Yous" or full partners is a common leadership concept. See, for example, Block, P., (2013). *Stewardship: Choosing Service Over Self-Interest*. San Francisco, CA: Jossey-Bass.

It is the wise leader who understands that **being patient, kind, and understanding and working for employees' best interests** will ultimately pay off by building **long-term trust and commitment.**

2. Developing Characteristics of Kindness Requires the Awareness of a Leader's Self-Interest

It is the wise leader who understands that being patient, kind, and understanding and working for employees' best interests will ultimately pay off by building long-term trust and commitment[211].

Being kind is **not successfully "faked"** and employees quickly **discern the difference between authentic and inauthentic leadership** qualities. Authentic and **genuine caring demands truly valuing others** and recognizing their worth.

[211] Beer, M., (2009), *op. cit.*

3. Kindness Is Ultimately a Reflection of a Leader's True Identity

Being kind is not "faked" and employees quickly discern the difference between authentic and inauthentic leadership qualities[212]. Authentic and genuine caring demands truly valuing others and recognizing their worth[213].

There is a **sacred and moral quality** in genuine leadership. Leadership is a **"covenantal" obligation of profound responsibility** to a multitude of stakeholders.

4. Treating Others Kindly Is a Distinctly Moral Obligation That Accompanies the Mantle of Leadership

There is a sacred and moral quality in genuine leadership. Leadership is a "covenantal" obligation of profound responsibility to a multitude of stakeholders. It is never to be taken lightly and being kind to others simply demonstrates the leader's understanding of her/his moral obligations[214].

---

212 Atwijuka, S., and Caldwell, C. (2017). "Authentic Leadership and the Ethic of Care." *Journal of Management Development*, Vol. 36, Iss. 8, pp. 1040-1051.

213 *Ibid.*

214 DePree, M., (2004), *op. cit.* and Covey, S. R., (2004), *op. cit.*

As leaders, or those who seek to become leaders, **examine themselves** and the challenges which their **responsibilities require of them**, they would do well to recognize that leadership and authority are **not granted to them by their rank or position**

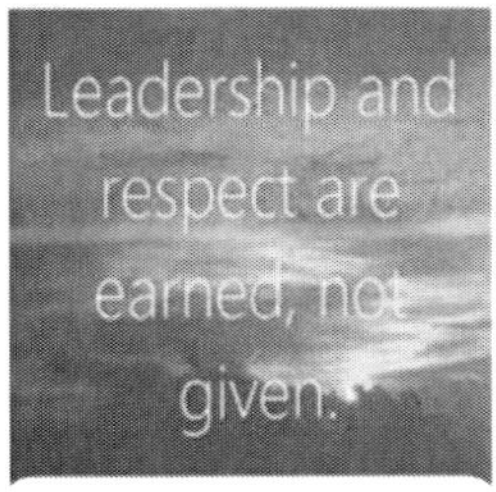

As leaders, or those who seek to become leaders, examine themselves and the challenges which their responsibilities require of them, they would do well to recognize that leadership and authority are not granted to them by their rank or position[215]. Leaders ultimately must earn the right to be trusted, followed, and respected[216]. Although kindness is not the only virtue required for leaders to earn the followership of others, it is a quality that those same followers will quickly respect. When leaders lack kindness, they are unlikely to ever be fully trusted.

Creating organizations with **aligned human resource management policies that honor employees, treat them with high trust, and empower employees** – rather than isolating and minimizing their contributions – have been **demonstrated to be critical to the establishment of high trust and the implementation of high-performance** work systems.

---

[215] This critically important point about leadership and authority is the key message of the most quoted of all management texts, Barnard, C. I., (1938). *The Functions of the Executive*. Cambridge, MA: Harvard College.

[216] *Ibid.*

More significant than its importance as a key to earning the followership of others, however, those who lead with kind hearts and a commitment to others' interests demonstrate the noble qualities that enable them to more completely fulfil their identities. True kindness and great leadership ultimately have their roots in the humble awareness that great things are possible when people work together in partnership together[217]. As leaders at all levels of an organization demonstrate their commitment to each other, they do so best when they are genuinely kind and committed to each other's welfare – and by so doing they benefit one another and help to make a better world[218].

---

[217] Anderson, V. and Caldwell, C., (Eds.). (2018). *Humility as Enlightened Leadership*. Hauppage, New York: NOVA Publishing.

[218] *Ibid.*

Chapter 6

LEADERSHIP AND GENEROSITY: THE GIVING OF ONESELF

According to the research of Jim Collins in his outstanding book, *Good to Great*, leaders in organizations that have transitioned from profitable to outstanding willingly give credit to others for their organizations' success and give generously of themselves to benefit others[219]. This personal example and giving spirit inspire greater personal commitment and encourage others to look within themselves to emulate their leaders' behaviors – two widely recognized benefits that link effective leadership and a leader's generosity.

This personal example and giving spirit **inspire greater personal commitment and encourage others to look within themselves** to emulate their leaders' behaviors – two widely recognized benefits that **link effective leadership and a leader's generosity.**

[219] See the findings about the qualities of Level 5 Leaders in Collins, J., (2001). *Good to Great: Why Some Companies Make the Leap . . . And Others Don't.* New York: HarperCollins.

The focus of this chapter is on the precise nature of generosity as a leadership quality. The chapter begins by defining generosity and citing six ways in which a leader's generosity positively influences others in organizations. The chapter then contrasts personal generosity with greed – the antithesis of a generous heart. Citing the inspiring example of David Packard, the co-founder with William Hewlett of the multinational information technology company that bears their names, the chapter briefly describes Packard's personal example of leadership and the generosity throughout his life for which he was known.

Turning to a contrasting example, the chapter then describes an individual whose values are the opposite of Packard's and who has been often cited as a person whose greed and self-interest have generated for him a fortune – but at the cost of literally billions of dollars in lost value both within the United States and internationally. The chapter then concludes with four insights about generosity for readers who seek to become more effective leaders by incorporating generosity within their own lives.

To be generous is to **recognize the needs of others and to make those needs a personal priority.** Simone de Beauvoir, the French philosopher, observed that **true generosity occurred when a person gave the full measure of himself or herself** – yet did so **feeling as if their actions cost them nothing.**

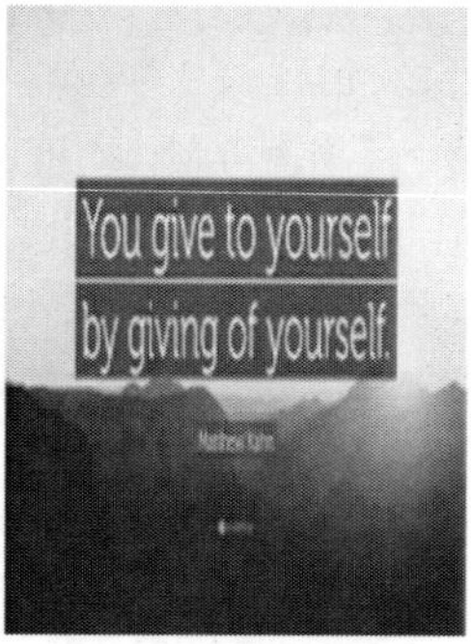

Leadership and Generosity

Generosity has been defined as "giving good things to others freely and abundantly[220]." To be generous is to recognize the needs of others and to

[220] This definition comes from the Notre Dame University "Science of Generosity" project found online on December 13, 2019 at https://generosityresearch.nd.edu/.

make those needs a personal priority[221]. Simone de Beauvoir, the French philosopher, observed that true generosity occurred when a person gave the full measure of himself or herself – yet did so feeling as if their actions cost them nothing[222].

Similarly, Jacques Cousteau suggested that generosity opens the way to wholeness and connection with others[223] and generosity has been called "*the most natural outward expression of an inner attitude of compassion and loving-kindness*[224]." Although we live in a world where generosity is often acknowledged to be a virtuous quality, the unfortunate reality is that many individuals who have been greatly blessed with abundance choose not to share that which they have with others.

Those who give out of no expectation of return choose to do so because of their belief that **those actions which benefit others carries with them their own reward.** In fact, those who give generously of themselves **view life as about service to others, personal sacrifice** to achieve a noble outcome, and **sharing to create a legacy of love.**

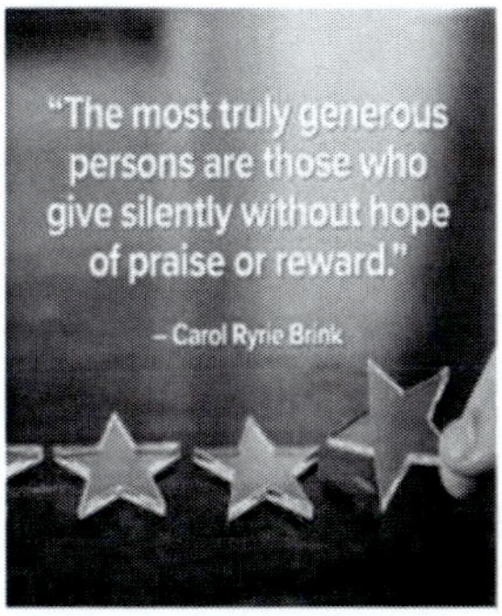

Generosity and giving of oneself to benefit others have been described as a key element of effective interpersonal relationships[225]. The logic of

---

221 Bernhard, T., (2014). "20 Quotations on Generosity: A Profound Act of Kindness." *Psychology Today*, August 31, 2014 and found online on December 12, 2019 at https://www.psychologytoday.com/us/blog/turning-straw-gold/201408/20-quotations-generosity-profound-act-kindness.

222 See "Simone de Beauvoir Quotes," *AZ Quotes*. Found online on December 12, 2019 at https://www.azquotes.com/author/1105-Simone_de_Beauvoir.

223 "Jacques-Yves Cousteau Quotes." BrainyQuote. Found online on December 12, 2019 at https://www.brainyquote.com/quotes/jacques_yves_cousteau_204389.

224 "Dalai Lama Quotes about Generosity." *AZ Quotes*. Found online on December 12, 2019 at https://www.azquotes.com/author/8418-Dalai_Lama/tag/generosity.

225 Munro, I. & Thanem, T., (2018). "The Ethics of Affective Leadership: Organizing Good Encounters Without Leaders." *Business Ethics Quarterly*, Vol. 28, Iss. 1, pp. 51-69.

giving to others generously transcends both the ethic of exchange and the ethic of duty[226]. Those who give out of no expectation of return choose to do so because of their belief that those actions which benefit others carry with them their own reward[227]. In fact, those who give generously of themselves view life as about service to others, personal sacrifice to achieve a noble outcome, and sharing to create a legacy of love[228].

Generosity becomes **an elite form of kindness, self-sacrifice, and concern** for others that is **freely given out of a desire to genuinely serve.** A leader's **generous actions stem from a unique inner truth** that is found deep within – a realization that **the role of leadership is to give of oneself to others so that others might benefit.**

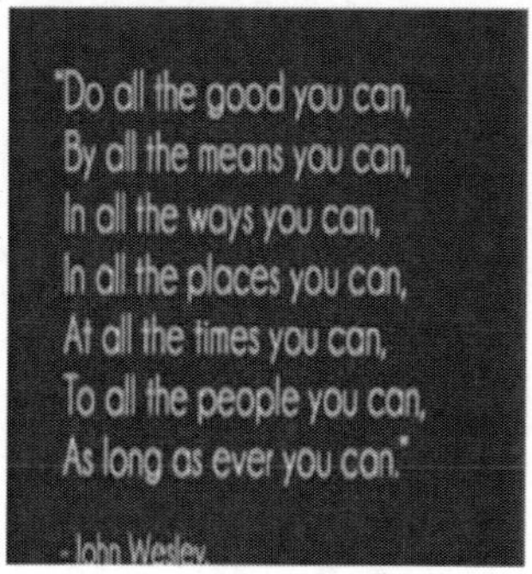

Generosity, then, is a virtuous choice. Generosity becomes an elite form of kindness, self-sacrifice, and concern for others that is freely given out of a desire to genuinely serve[229]. A leader's generous actions stem from a unique inner truth that is found deep within – a realization that the role of leadership is to give of oneself to others so that others might benefit[230]. Sometimes labeled "prosocial behavior" or "cooperation," acts of generosity are not uncommon and reflect an inner propensity in many people[231].

---

226 Baviera, T., English, W. & Guillen, M., (2016). "The 'Logic of Gift" Inspiring Behavior in Organizations Beyond the Limits of Duty and Exchange." *Business Ethics Quarterly,* Vol. 26, Iss. 2, pp. 159-180.

227 *Ibid.*

228 Connor, T., (2018). "Who Lives in Life? Givers or Takers. The One Thing That Separates Them is Their Outlook on Life." *Personal Excellence Essentials*, Vol. 23, Iss.6, pp. 9-10.

229 Bernhard, T., (2014), *op. cit."*

230 Sudbrink, L., (2016) "Leveraging GRIT for Leadership Success." *Leader to Leader*, Vol. 2016, Iss. 79, pp. 57-62.

231 Allen, S., (2018). "The Science of Generosity." John Templeton Foundation, .Greater Good Science Center, University of California at Berkeley found online on December 13, 2019 at https://ggsc.berkeley.edu/images/uploads/GGSC-JTF_White_Paper-Generosity-FINAL.pdf.

The irony and paradox of generosity is that those who give freely of themselves actually increase the quality of their own lives.

The irony and paradox of generosity is that those who give freely of themselves actually increase the quality of their own lives[232]. According to Christian Smith and Hilary Davidson, generosity improves personal well-being and the quality of one's life in five specific ways[233].

Personal Happiness

The scholarly research confirms that individuals who tithe, or who give away at least 10% of their income to others on an annual basis, perceive themselves as happier than comparable individuals who do not share their resources[234]. In addition, research about volunteerism indicates that the more hours per month in which a person is involved in volunteer service, the happier a person will self-describe how (s)he feels[235].

Bodily Health

Ground-breaking research about generosity and its impact on the brain indicates that generosity improves bodily health by reducing both stress and

---

[232] This powerful point is made in Smith, C. & Davidson, H. (2014). The Paradox of Generosity. New York: Oxford University Press.
[233] *Ibid.* These five points are found on page 13 of their book.
[234] *Ibid.* See page 15.
[235] *Ibid.* found on page 17.

anxiety[236]. Research about altruism within a work context has also been found to improve personal well-being and commitment[237].

Ground-breaking research about generosity and its impact on the brain indicates that **generosity improves bodily health by reducing both stress and anxiety.** Research about **altruism within a work context** has also been found to **improve personal well-being and commitment.**

Purpose in Living

An extensive study conducted over many years by the University of Wisconsin found that the desire to help others had a significant impact on overall life satisfaction[238]. People are generous and give of themselves to others because they believe that doing so helps them to fulfill their personal identities while honoring others and their potential[239].

People are generous and **give of themselves to others** because they believe that **doing so** helps them **to fulfill their personal identities** while **honoring others and their potential.**

---

[236] Inagaki, T. E. & Ross, L. P., (2018). "Neural Correlates of Giving Social Support: Differences Between Giving Targeted and Untargeted Support." Preprint found on December 13, 2019 at https://psyarxiv.com/eudqf/,

[237] Moynihan, D. P., DeLeire, T., & Kohei, E., (2013). "A Life Worth Living: Evidence on the Relationship Between Prosocial Values and Happiness." Found online on December 13, 2019 at https://pdfs.semanticscholar.org/1d7f/30c6f99ad400579fe24eac4c3cdfefdcd7c8.pdf?_ga=2.79721879.1693506563.1576256574-1463184506.1576256574 and published in the *American Review of Public Administration* in 2015.

[238] *Ibid.*

[239] This important point is made in Covey, S. R., (2004). The 8th Habit: From Effectiveness to Greatness. New York: Free Press.

Avoidance of Depression

Generosity is a deterrent to depression. It shifts one's focus off oneself and the problems that one faces and enables a person to change a negative lens about oneself into a more positive focus[240], In addition, being generous promotes mental health, reduces stress and supports the immune system [241].

Interest in Personal Growth

People who are generous with others look more positively at themselves and at the world[242]. Generosity is "a natural confidence builder and a natural repellent of self-hatred[243]." The sensitivity shown to others makes it easier to value oneself[244]. In addition, the experience of being generous to others reinforces one's belief that (s)he can become a better person and strengthens the desire to do just that[245].

The sensitivity shown to others **makes it easier to value oneself.** In addition, the experience of **being generous to others reinforces one's belief that (s)he can become a better person and strengthens the desire to do just that**.

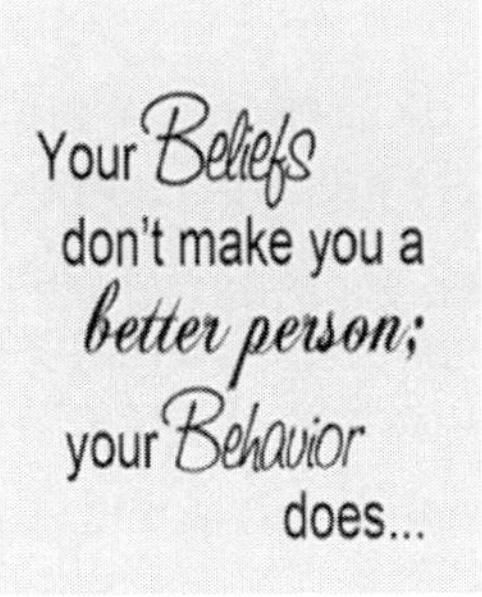

These five benefits are a testament to the importance of the principle advocated by many individuals that serving others brings its own rewards – and is, in fact, a moral obligation with residual benefits. Those who promote

---

[240] Firestone, L., (2010). "Generosity: What's In It for You?" Psychology Today, November 24, 2010 and found online on December 13, 2019 at https://ggsc.berkeley.edu/images/uploads/GGSC-JTF_White_Paper-Generosity-FINAL.pdf.

[241] *Ibid.*

[242] *Ibid.*

[243] *Ibid.*

[244] *Ibid.*

[245] Moynihan, D. P., DeLeire, T., & Kohei, E., (2013), *op. cit.*

generosity as a philosophy of life describe it as a unique form of personal self-interest that benefits both those who receive and the giver.

Those who promote generosity as a **philosophy of life** describe it as **a unique form of personal self-interest** that benefits both **those who receive and the giver**.

GREED AND SELFISHNESS

In contrast with generosity, the qualities of greed and selfishness are rarely associated with the qualities of an effective leader – with the possible exception of the fictional Wall Street movie character, Gordon Gekko[246]. Greed is widely understood as the intense personal quest for money, power, or other selfish interest – but the Roman poet, Horace, suggested that it was never satisfied[247].

Like selfishness, greed is concerned with personal self-interest. Ironically, however, the Ethic of Self-Interest affirms that the wisest course for those who wish to succeed is to focus on long-term wealth creation rather than short-term gain[248].

---

[246] Gordon Gekko alleged, of course, that "Greed is good" and his monologue in the movie, Wall Street, parodied the greed of many financial entrepreneurs.

[247] See "The Best Quotes about Greed" *Ranker,com* found online on December 15, 2019 at https://www.ranker.com/list/notable-and-famous-greed-quotes/reference.

[248] This point is well made by Hosmer, L. T., (1995). "Trust: The Connecting Link Between Organizational Theory and Philosophical Ethics." *Academy of Management Review*, Vol. 20, Iss. 2, pp. 379-403 and Caldwell, C. and Atwijuka, S., (2019). "Self-Examination and the Ethic of Self-Interest." Paper accepted for publication in the *Journal of Values-Based Leadership.*

Like selfishness, greed is concerned with personal self-interest. Ironically, however, the Ethic of Self-Interest affirms that the wisest course for those who wish to succeed is to focus on long-term wealth creation rather than short-term gain.

Many believe that truly successful people focus on serving others while those who are unsuccessful simply seek a short-term benefit and ask, "What's in it for me?[249]" Unfortunately, there are at least an equal number who seek that which they perceive will personally benefit them – to the detriment of others and society. It is this tendency that caused former New York Congresswoman, Shirley Chisholm to observe that "(w)hen morality comes up against profit, it is seldom that profit loses[250]."

Unfortunately, there are at least an equal number who seek that which they perceive will personally benefit them – to the detriment of others and society. It is this tendency that caused former New York Congresswoman, Shirley Chisholm to observe that "(w)hen morality comes up against profit, it is seldom that profit loses.

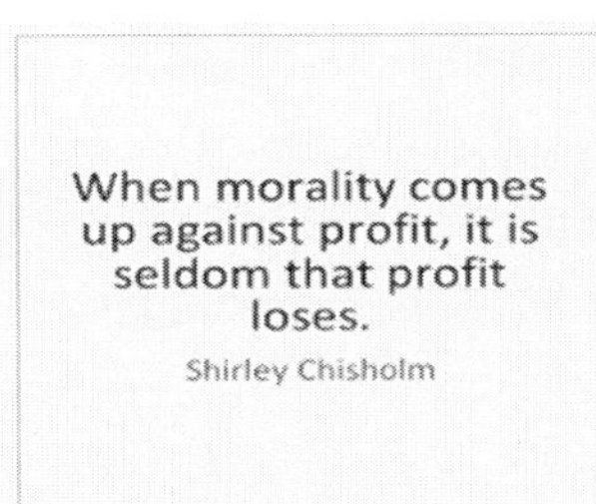

---

[249] See the quote from Brian Tracy at "Greed Quotes." Goodreads. Found online on December 15, 2019 at https://www.goodreads.com/quotes/tag/greed.

[250] "Shirley Chisholm Quotes." AZ Quotes. Found online on December 15, 2019 at https://www.azquotes.com/author/2825-Shirley_Chisholm.

The Pulitzer Prize winning political commentator and author, Thomas. L. Friedman has noted that it is typically greed and warped personal self-interest that has often been the cause of many detriments to society[251]. That self-interest, although typically misperceived, can nonetheless have a devastating impact upon others. Erich Fromm is among several observers who has noted that one of the major problems of those who are motivated by greed is that their desires are never satisfied[252].

Erich Fromm is among several observers who has noted that one of the major problems of **those who are motivated by greed** is that their desires are **never satisfied**.

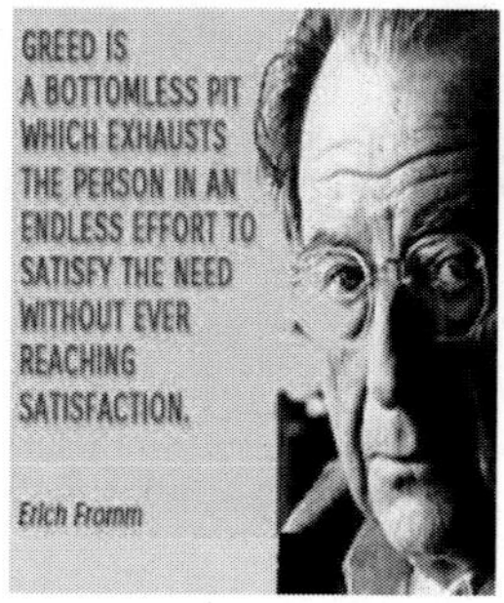

David Packard: Exemplar of Generosity

David Packard, co-founder of the greatly successful Hewlett-Packard Company, was nonetheless a modest and simple man – and a benefactor to many. He and his wife, Lucille, were believers in philanthropy and public service well before he and Bill Hewlett transformed the small electric shop in a garage to one of America's greatest companies[253]. Packard believed that a company had a moral obligation to produce value for society, explaining that generating profits "is not the proper end and aim of management - it is what makes all of the proper ends and aims possible[254]."

---

[251] Friedman, T. L., (2009). *Hot, Flat, and Crowded: Why We Need a Green Revolution – And How It Can Renew America, Release 2.0*. New York: Picador Press.

[252] "Erich Fromm Quotes about Greed." *AZ Quotes*. Found online on December 15, 2019 at https://www.azquotes.com/author/5198-Erich_Fromm/tag/greed.

[253] See "Our History." *The David and Lucille Packard Foundation*. Found online on December 13, 2019 at https://www.packard.org/about-the-foundation/our-history/.

[254] "David Packard Quotes" AZ Quotes. Found online on December 13, 2019 at https://www.azquotes.com/author/11226-David_Packard.

Packard believed that a company had a **moral obligation to produce value for society,** explaining that generating profits "is not the proper end and aim of management - it is **what makes all of the proper ends and aims possible.**"

Packard believed that an organization has "a responsibility to its employees, to its customers, and to the community at large" – and Packard honored that obligation by pioneering "many innovative benefits and management concepts, such as flexible working hours, catastrophic medical coverage, and open offices[255]." Among his most famous quotations, Packard is known for believing that "the betterment of society is not a job to be left to a few. It's a responsibility to be shared by all[256]" Packard exemplified those words, taking a break from serving as the Chairman of the Board at Hewlett-Packard during the Nixon administration to serve as Nixon's Deputy Secretary of Defense[257].

Packard is known for believing that "**the betterment of society** is not a job to be left to a few. It's **a responsibility to be shared by all.**"

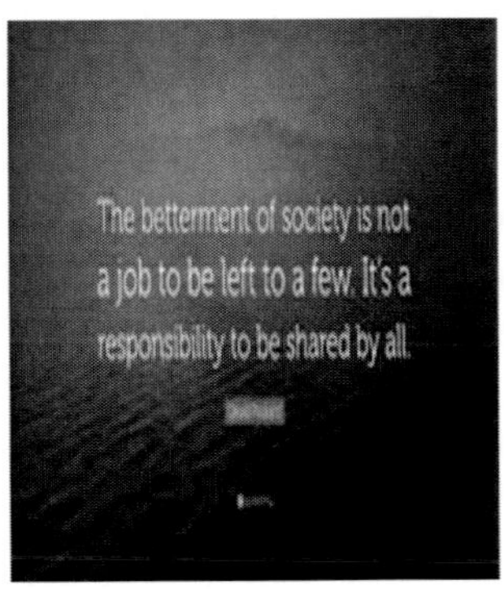

---

255 *Ibid.*

256 *Ibid.*

257 For a summary of Packard's timeline, see Packard, D. (2006). *The HP Way: How Bill Hewlett and I Built Our Company*. New York: HarperCollins.

Jim Collins called David Packard one of the top ten Chief Executive Officers of all time. Of Packard, Jim Collins wrote the following tribute:

> Despite being one of Silicon Valley's first self-made billionaires, he lived in the same small house that he and his wife built for themselves in 1957, overlooking a simple orchard. The tiny kitchen, with its dated linoleum and the simply furnished living room bespoke a man who needed no material symbols to proclaim "I'm a billionaire. I'm important. I'm successful." "His idea of a good time," said Bill Terry, who worked with Packard for thirty-six years," was to get some friends together to string some barbed wire." Packard bequeathed his $5.6 billion estate to a charitable foundation and, upon his death, his family created a eulogy pamphlet, with a photo of him sitting on a tractor in farming clothes. The caption made no reference to his status as one of the great industrialists of the twentieth century. It simply read, "David Packard, 1912-1996, Rancher, etc."

Understated and humblc, David Packard exemplified a leader who cared more about what he was to contribute to the world than to acquire for himself. In a tribute to David Packard after his death, Joel Birnbaum wrote that "Dave Packard was one of the richest men in the United States and also among the most generous[258]."

Understated and humble, David Packard exemplified a leader who cared more about what he was to contribute to the world than to acquire for himself. In a tribute to David Packard after his death, Joel Birnbaum wrote that "Dave Packard was one of the richest men in the United States and also among the most generous."

DAVID PACKARD

---

[258] See page 214 of Birnbaum, J., (2001). *Memorial Tributes, Volume 9 (2001)*. Washington, D.C.: National Academies Press.

ANOTHER PERSPECTIVE

One of the individuals considered to be a major contributor to the 2007 fiscal crisis and who exemplified unsatiated greed is the perpetuator of the Abacus financial instrument. The 2007 -2008 financial crisis was precipitated by a liquidity shortfall in the U.S. banking system due to the virtual collapse of the subprime mortgage market[259].

Ironically, this financial crisis was substantially aided by the creation of a financial instrument developed and promoted by one of America's most wealthy billionaires and its largest financial firm. The firm was eventually fined more than $500 million for its role in creating and marketing a financial instrument virtually guaranteed to collapse.

The 2007-2008 financial crisis was precipitated by a **liquidity shortfall in the U.S. banking system due to the virtual collapse of the subprime mortgage market.** Ironically, this financial crisis was substantially **by the creation of a financial instrument developed and promoted by one of America's most wealthy billionaires** and its largest financial firm.

Financial Crisis Worldwide

The individual who was the mastermind behind this scenario was a Harvard graduate, and a hedge fund billionaire. Despite knowing the impact that these financial machinations would have on the world economic market, this individual carefully selected high risk investments in creating a financial instrument that was guaranteed to fail, then sold the instrument short in the investment bond market.

---

[259] For more about the 2007 fiscal crisis, see Whalen, P., (2019). "Goldman Sachs and the ABACUS Deal." Seven Pillars Institute. Kansas City, MO. Found online on December 15, 2019 at https://sevenpillarsinstitute.org/case-studies/goldman-sachs-and-the-abacus-deal/.

Despite knowing the impact that these financial machinations would have on the world economic market, this individual **carefully selected high risk investments in creating a financial instrument that was guaranteed to fail,** then sold the instrument short in the investment bond market.

This person and the investment company each made $2 billion in profits as a result. Not content to be a multi-billionaire with wealth unimagined by most individuals, this person then made the decision to relocate his financial portfolio from the United States to Puerto Rico to avoid U.S. tax liabilities. The 2007-2008 fiscal crisis had worldwide financial implications, plunging the world economy in the worst economic depression since The Great Depression of 1929[260].

This person and the investment company made $2 billion in profits as a result. **Not content to be a multi-billionaire** with wealth unimagined by most individuals, this person then **made the decision to relocate his financial portfolio from the United States to Puerto Rico to avoid U.S. tax** liabilities.

Apparently, $2 billion was just not enough!

The reverberations in the world economy generated by this crisis continues to impact many nations of the world and cost individuals throughout the world billions of dollars in financial losses. Meanwhile, the individual responsible for creating the financial instrument which played a major part in causing this financial debacle avoided personal legal

---

[260] Friedman, T. L., (2009), *op. cit.*

prosecution – though his name is considered anathema by many investors throughout the world and he has been the subject of dozens of articles that have cited him as the real world equivalent of Wall Street's worst example.

> Meanwhile, **the individual responsible** for creating the financial instrument which played a major part in causing this financial debacle **avoided personal legal prosecution** – though his name is **considered anathema by many investors throughout the world** and he has been **the subject of dozens of articles that have cited him as the real world equivalent of Wall Street's worst example.**

Insights about Generosity

As applied to the role of leaders and as a quality that would-be leaders should consider emulating, generosity merits thoughtful consideration. The following are four significant insights about the relationship between leadership and generosity.

1. Generosity Earns a Greater Commitment from Others

By their positive example, leaders who demonstrate generosity in the ways that they live and in their dealings with others tend to see their example followed by those with whom they work. Generosity on the part of an organization's leaders is reciprocated and emulated by managers, supervisors and employees[261].

---

[261] Virtuous behaviors of leaders are consistently respected and are more likely to be adopted by others. See Covey, S. R., (2004), *op. cit.*

By their positive example, leaders who demonstrate generosity in the ways that they live and in their dealings with others tend to **see their example followed** by those with whom they work. Generosity on the part of an organization's leaders is **reciprocated and emulated by managers, supervisors and employees.**

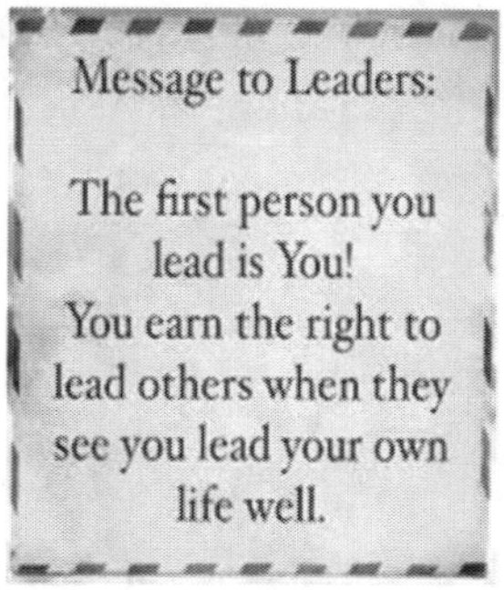

2. Generosity Builds Organizational Good Will

Leaders who model generosity create organizational cultures that are positive and that earn the trust of customers, regulating agencies, and the general public. The good will acquired by leaders who are generous is responded to outside of the organization as well as within it[262].

Leaders who model generosity **create organizational cultures that are positive and that earn the trust** of customers, regulating agencies, and the general public. The **good will** acquired by leaders who are generous is **responded to outside of the organization as well as within** it.

LEADERS WHO MODEL THE WAY EARN RESPECT

3. Generosity Honors a Moral Responsibility

Generosity is perceived as morally responsible and is consistent with the mantra, "Service is the rent we pay for living in this world." Generosity is

---

262 Pfeffer, J., (1998), *op. cit.*

believed to be an acknowledgement of the fact that the world has provided the opportunity for an organization to succeed. Repaying that opportunity by being generous is viewed as an ethical obligation[263].

Generosity is **perceived as morally responsible** and is consistent with the mantra, **"Service is the rent we pay for living on this earth."** Generosity is believed to be an **acknowledgement of the fact that the world has provided the opportunity** for an organization to succeed.

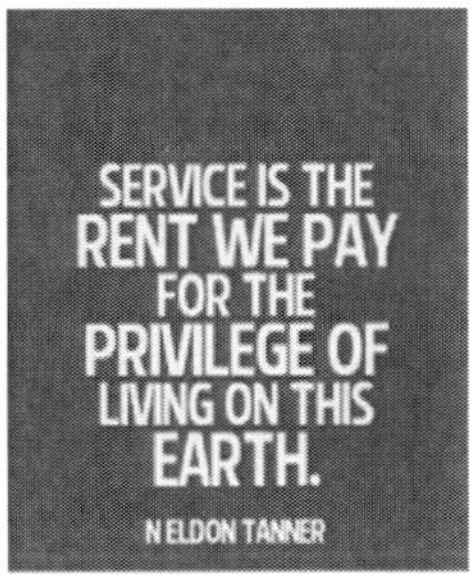

4. Generosity Makes Life More Satisfying

Leaders who exemplify generosity enjoy the accompanying benefits of better health, a more satisfying life, and less stress. These leaders also feel greater personal self-regard and tend to be both happier and more at peace[264].

Leaders who exemplify generosity enjoy the accompanying benefits of **better health, a more satisfying life, and less stress.** These leaders also feel **greater personal self-regard** and tend to be both **happier and more at peace.**

[263] Friedman, T. L., (2009), *op. cit.*
[264] Bernhard, T., (2014), *op. cit.*

Each of these four insights affirms the importance of leaders, or those who seek to become leaders, adopting the qualities of generosity – not only because of the benefits to them and to their organization but because generosity brings to individuals a higher quality of life for themselves, as well as for those around them.

CONCLUSION

Both David Packard and his antithesis as a leader provide powerful insights about the importance of the leader's role in organization – and the likelihood that a leader will be viewed by others in a light that is either good or bad. Notably, both Packard and his counterpart were extremely successful individuals who accomplished amazing results and whose record of achievement is unusual.

The contrast between the two men, however, is remarkable and profound. Packard is a man who **devoted his life to adding value for the world and his legacy is entirely positive.** While the other individual was financially successful, he is generally **regarded with disdain by a world who views him as selfish – if not profoundly immoral.**

The contrast between the two men, however, is remarkable and profound. Packard is a man who devoted his life to adding value for the world and his legacy is entirely positive. While the other individual was financially successful, he is generally regarded with disdain by a world who view him as selfish – if not profoundly immoral. The great benefit of generosity for those who seek to lead is that the values of service, giving to others, and contributing to society's welfare accompany the generous leader – as well as greater commitment and respect from others and greater personal satisfaction.

Chapter 7

FEMININE LEADERSHIP AND ITS STRENGTHS

Despite the patterned stereotyping of women as "too emotional" or "indecisive," **recent empirical evidence suggests that female leaders have distinct advantages** over their male counterparts – particularly under specific conditions **when collaborative and cooperative organizational responses are necessary.**

The concept of the "glass ceiling" has been a barrier for women for centuries – although the past thirty years have brought a measurable improvement in opportunities for women to serve as corporate executives and in other leadership roles[265]. Despite the patterned stereotyping of women as "too emotional" or "indecisive," recent empirical evidence suggests that female leaders have distinct advantages over their male counterparts –

---

[265] Lewis, J. J., (2019). "The Glass Ceiling and Women's History: An Invisible Barrier to Success," ThoughtCo., August 18, 2019 and found online on December 17, 2019 at https://www.thoughtco.com/glass-ceiling-for-women-definition-3530823.

particularly under specific conditions when collaborative and cooperative organizational responses are necessary.

The purpose of this chapter is to examine the advantages of the feminine leadership style, acknowledging in advance that there is no definitive leadership approach that applies to every woman. Acknowledging that there is often as much or more difference in leadership characteristics among women than there is between men and women, this chapter identifies general tendencies about the leadership approach that categorizes the interpersonal style of many women who serve in leadership positions.

The specific advantages of the feminine leadership style are described in context with the requirements of today's modern organizations.

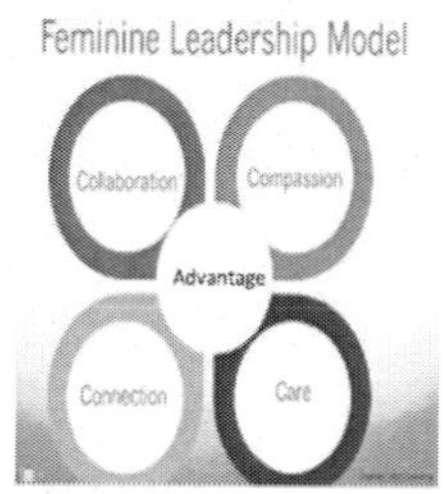

The specific advantages of the feminine leadership style, along with potential vulnerabilities that are associated with feminine leadership, are described in context with the requirements of today's modern organizations. Following that introduction, the leadership style and significant accomplishments of Florence Nightingale, known as the Mother of Modern Nursing, are described as an example of an outstanding female leader who successfully utilizes key qualities of the feminine leadership model.

An example of a leader who fails to successfully incorporate feminine leadership attributes is then presented as a contrasting example. The chapter then suggests six insights about feminine leadership that bear replicating by the leaders of the modern organization, and concludes with a challenge to leaders to develop and refine the skills that typify the feminine leadership model.

FEMININE LEADERSHIP MODEL

The well-documented cultural proclivity for masculine leadership and the blatant bias against women as leaders is a widely-acknowledged artefact of many cultures worldwide[266]. Jironet has suggested that women have been excluded from the conversation, been silenced, and not been taken seriously as potential leaders due to stereotype, superstition, and ideological agendas[267]. For whatever the root cause reasons, the acknowledged reality is that the feminine leadership model is often viewed as sub-standard by many individuals – despite the fact that a growing body of evidence suggests an entirely different story[268].

For whatever the root cause reasons, the acknowledged reality is that **the feminine leadership model is often viewed as sub-standard** by many individuals – **despite the fact that a growing body of evidence suggests an entirely different story.**

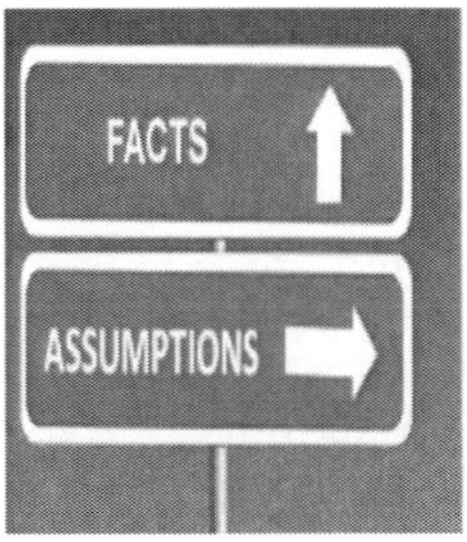

Although the persons responsible for perpetuating the stereotypical bias for "white male" leadership at the outset of the industrial revolution were simply reflecting the cultural assumptions of that time, the impact of their perspectives has continued to influence the work world for more than a century[269]. Typical of the perspectives of history literally for millennia, the

---

[266] Gray, C., (2019). "It's a Man's World . . . Or Is It? Finding a Seat at the Table for Feminine Leadership." *Leadership Excellence*, Vol. 36, Iss. 9, pp. 5-7.

[267] Jironet, K. (2019). *Feminine Leadership: Personal Development Beyond Polarities*. New York: Routledge.

[268] For example, see the work of Martin Chemers in Chemers, M., (2014). *An Integrative Theory of Leadership*. London, UK: Psychology Press.

[269] Gray, C., (2019), *op. cit.*

biases about gender and leadership have constantly influenced opportunities for women to demonstrate their unique abilities. According to a McKinsey/LeanIn.Org study, 48% of all new hires in organizations are now women, but women are uniformly underrepresented in top management roles[270].

Deborah Tannen has written extensively about the **variance in how men and women communicate** and Carol Gilligan has described in detail **the distinctive ways that differentiate the male and the female moral perspective.**

Not the Same

Deborah Tannen has written extensively about the variance in how men and women communicate[271] and Carol Gilligan has described in detail the distinctive ways that differentiate the male and the female moral perspective[272]. Examining these differences, as well as other ways in which men and women tend to relate to others interpersonally, within organizations, and as members of society offers powerful evidence regarding the nature of feminine leadership and its important qualities.

One approach to the feminine leadership model suggests that "women value and excel in consensus-building, cooperation, nurturance, charisma, and interpersonal relations more than do men[273]." Tannen noted that the

---

[270] Cited in Love, A., (2018). "Leveraging the Power of Feminine Leadership." *PA Times*, Vol. 4, Iss. 2, pp. 37-38.

[271] Tannen's excellent work is found in many books. See, for example, Tannen, D., (2007). *You Just Don't Understand: Women and Men in Conversation*. New York: HarperCollins.

[272] Gilligan's superb assessment of how women view moral priorities is found in several places. See, for example, Gilligan, C., (2016). *In a Different Voice: Psychological Theory and Women's Development*. Boston, MA: Harvard University Press.

[273] Paris, L. D., Howell, J. P, Dorfman, P. W. & Hanges, P. J., (2009). "Preferred Leadership Prototypes of Male and Female Leaders in 27 Countries." *Journal of International Business Studies*, Vol. 40, pp. 1396–1405.

feminine communication style is more supportive, focused more on suggesting than telling, and centered on helping others rather than directing them[274]. According to a 2014 study of 6,500 respondents worldwide about leadership effectiveness, female leaders are rated superior to their male counterparts "in five out of seven metrics of effective leadership[275]." In four of the metrics, "leading by example," "communicating in an open and transparent way," "admitting mistakes," and "bringing out the best in others," more than half of the survey respondents felt that women leaders performed better than men and in a fifth metric, "handling controversial issues quietly and calmly," men and women were about equal with women ranking slightly better.

In four metrics, "**leading by example,**" "**communicating in an open and transparent way,**" "**admitting mistakes,**" and "**bringing out the best in others,**" more than half of the survey respondents felt that **women leaders performed better** than men and in a fifth metric, **"handling controversial issues quietly and calmly,"** men and women were about equal with **women ranking slightly better**.

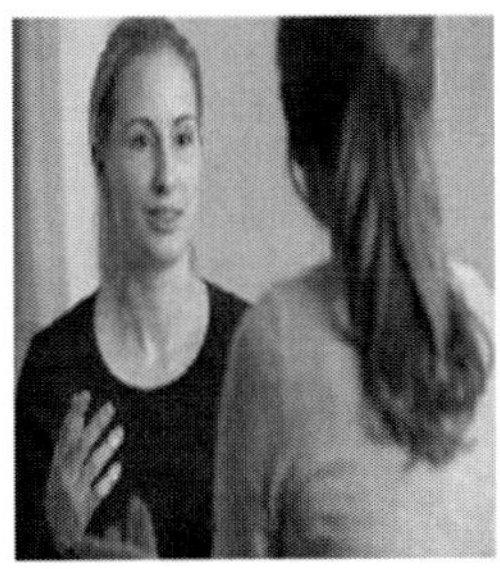

Although women often adopt masculine leadership traits in an attempt to compete in today's organizations, the evidence suggests that the feminine leadership style is far more effective[276]. Women who seek to adopt an assertive, authoritarian, and aggressive leadership style are sometimes labeled as a "Machiavellian Mary" and perceived to be "our worst bosses,"

---

[274] Tannen, D., (2007), *op. cit.*

[275] Dill, K., (2014). "The End of 'Macho'? Survey Identifies Feminine Leadership Communication as the Way of the Future." *Forbes.com*, p. 21, May 20, 2014 and found online on December 18, 2019 at https://www.forbes.com/sites/kathryndill/2014/05/20/the-end-of-macho-survey-identifies-feminine-leadership-communication-as-the-way-of-the-future/#76bdb8aa5b4d.

[276] Love, A., (2018), *op. cit.*

according to many of their employees[277]. Female leaders who adopt an "Iron Lady" approach to organizational leadership are prone to undermining the creativity and growth potential that a more supportive personal style can enhance[278].

Women who seek to **adopt an assertive, authoritarian, and aggressive leadership style** are sometimes labeled as a "Machiavellian Mary" and perceived to be "our worst bosses," according to many of their employees. Female leaders who adopt an "Iron Lady" approach to organizational leadership are **prone to undermining the creativity and growth potential** that a more supportive personal style can enhance.

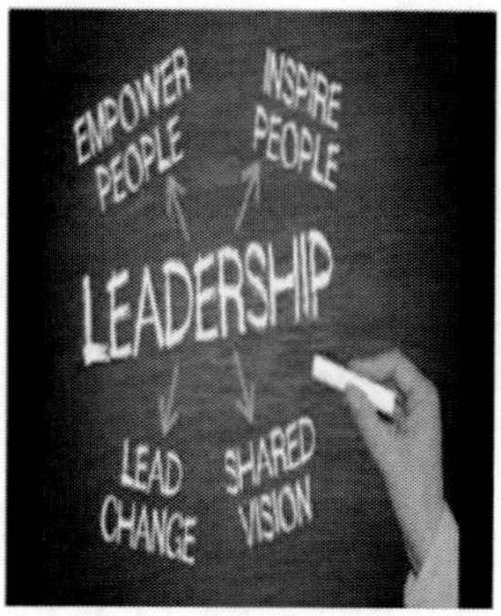

In characterizing the unique style of feminine leadership, Marilyn Loden, author of the book, *Feminine Leadership*, described the feminine leadership style as follows:

> "Feminine leaders rely heavily on intuition as well as rational thinking in solving problems. They focus more on long-term goals which are good for the entire organization as opposed to short-term. And they generally prefer a "win-win" approach to conflict resolution instead of the traditional "win-lose" approach[279]."

Although Loden emphasized that not all women followed this style and that this leadership style is not totally foreign to some men, she added that

---

[277] *Ibid.*

[278] *Ibid.*

[279] See page 472 of Loden, M., (1986). "Feminine Leadership: It Can Make Your Business More Profitable." *Vital Speeches of the Day*, Vol. 52, Iss. 15, pp. 472-473. Delivered at the Baltimore Business Leader Conference, Notre Dame College, Baltimore, Maryland, March 13, 1986.

women tend to exhibit these leadership qualities to a far greater degree than men[280].

Feminine leadership **emphasizes caring about others** and treats employees with **a commitment to their welfare.** Relationships are highly important, and **in an age when employee engagement is critical, feminine leadership is far more committed to involving employees** than their masculine counterparts. At the same time, feminine leadership is also **duty-focused and believes that honoring obligations also honors relationships** with others.

Feminine leadership also reflects the Ethic of Care, a feminine moral perspective[281] that differs significantly from Lawrence Kohlberg's traditional, rule-oriented, justice-based, masculine view of moral development[282]. Feminine leadership emphasizes caring about others and treats employees with a commitment to their welfare. Relationships are highly important, and in an age when employee engagement is critical, feminine leadership is far more committed to involving employees than their masculine counterparts[283]. At the same time, feminine leadership is also duty-focused and believes that honoring obligations also honors relationships with others[284].

The implicit differences between the ways that men and women tend to see the world have been widely acknowledged, and the value of diversity in perspectives has been broadly recognized, but little progress has been made in utilizing the contributions that can be made by incorporating the many

---

[280] *Ibid*, p. 472.
[281] Gilligan, C., (2016), *op. cit.*
[282] Kohlberg, L., (1981). *The Philosophy of Moral Development: Moral Stages and the Idea of Justice*. New York: Harper and Row.
[283] Paris, L. D., Howell, J. P, Dorfman, P. W. & Hanges, P. J., (2009), op. cit.
[284] Gilligan, C., (2016), *op. cit.*

strengths of feminine leadership and that are so badly needed in today's modern organizations[285].

FLORENCE NIGHTINGALE AND COMPASSIONATE SERVICE

From the time she was a young girl, Florence Nightingale felt a personal calling to serve others and to care for their needs[286]. Perhaps no other woman has been a better combination of effective administration, compassionate service, and unflagging personal commitment than Florence Nightingale[287]. Coming to prominence in the Crimean War because of her exceptional organizational skills, Florence Nightingale became a symbol of the contributions that a woman can make to improve the lives of others.

Perhaps **no other woman has been a better combination of effective administration, compassionate service, and unflagging personal commitment** than Florence Nightingale. Coming to prominence in the Crimean War because of her exceptional organizational skills, Florence Nightingale became **a symbol of the contributions that a woman can make** to improve the lives of others.

Brought up in the Victorian era when women of social status were not supposed to work in menial jobs, Nightingale defied her parents' wishes to honor what she believed to be a divine calling in nursing[288]. Nightingale used statistical analysis to collect data and systematize record keeping –

[285] *Ibid.*
[286] Hamilton, L. M. & North, W. (2015). *Florence Nightingale: A Life Inspired.* Sudbury, MA: Wyatt North Publishing.
[287] *Ibid.*
[288] "Florence Nightingale." *Biography.com* July 9, 2019 and found online on December 21, 2019 at https://www.biography.com/scientist/florence-nightingale.

demonstrating the need for more sanitary conditions in both the Crimean War and in the care given to patients within hospitals[289]. Nightingale believed totally in her calling and was deeply committed to the service of others – believing that the first requirement in a hospital is that it should do the sick no harm.

Brought up in the Victorian era when women of social status were not supposed to work in menial jobs, Nightingale defied her parents wishes **to honor what she believed to be a divine calling in nursing.** Nightingale used statistical analysis to collect data and systematize record keeping -- demonstrating the need for more **sanitary conditions** in both the Crimean War and in the **care given to patients** within hospitals.

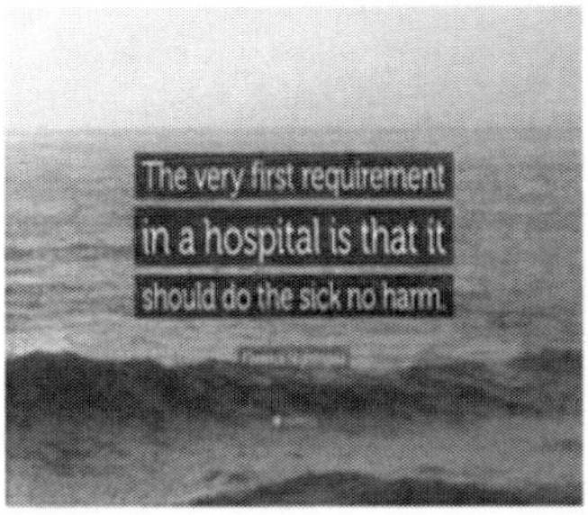

Deeply committed to her calling, Nightingale viewed herself as a servant to others and referenced her calling in reverent terms.

> "If I could give you information of my life it would be to show how a woman of very ordinary ability has been led by God in strange and unaccustomed paths to do in His service what He has done in her. And if I could tell you all, you would see how God has done all, and I nothing. I have worked hard, very hard, that is all; and I have never refused God anything[290]."

---

[289] Audain, C., (1998). "Florence Nightingale." *Biographies of Woman Mathematicians* found online on December 21, 2019 at https://www.agnesscott.edu/lriddle/women/nitegale.htm.

[290] "Florence Nightingale Quotes." *Goodreads*. Found online on December 21, 2019 at https://www.goodreads.com/author/quotes/63031.Florence_Nightingale.

At the same time, Nightingale opined that the leader's responsibility was to ensure that others followed correct principles and performed the duties to which they were appointed[291].

Nightingale demonstrated her ability to **improve the quality of nursing** by utilizing a knowledge of statistical methods to **bring analysis and order into nursing.** Nightingale **founded the first secular nursing school** in the world at the St. Thomas Hospital in London. An **innovative social reformer**, Nightingale was also a women's advocate in addition to initiating **healthcare reforms for all sectors of society** in England.

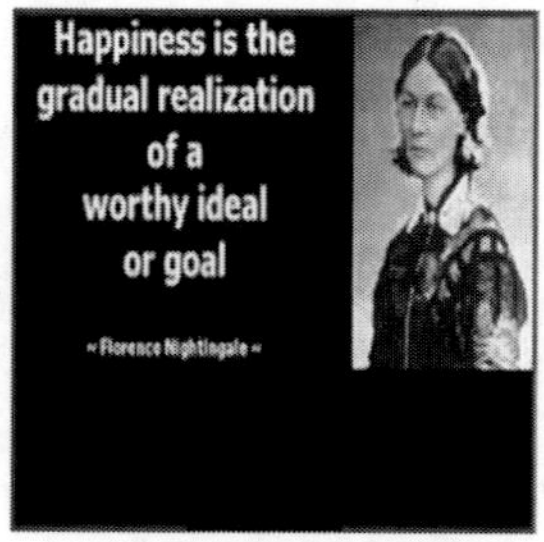

Nightingale demonstrated her ability to improve the quality of nursing by utilizing a knowledge of statistical methods to bring analysis and order into nursing. Nightingale founded the first secular nursing school in the world at the St. Thomas Hospital in London. An innovative social reformer, Nightingale was also a women's advocate in addition to initiating healthcare reforms for all sectors of society in England.

INEFFECTIVE LEADERSHIP

This "leader" established a reputation for being a "black widow" – known throughout the university for **destroying the careers of many subordinates** and terminating individuals who worked for her.

[291] *Ibid.*

A classic example of a woman with an ineffective leadership style is an individual who adopted a condescending approach to others, relying on her positional power and her family relationship with the president of the university where she worked to dominate and criticize other individuals who worked for her. This particular individual was able to maintain her position for a number of years, principally because her brother was the University President and was personally highly regarded.

Although this woman was nominally successful in maintaining her position for several years, she was feared by those with whom she worked and given lip service rather than a full personal commitment from others who worked for her. This "leader" established a reputation for being a "black widow" – known throughout the university for destroying the careers of many subordinates and terminating individuals who worked for her. Because of her relationship with the university president, her conduct was tolerated – despite the fact that many in the organization considered her to be both an ineffective leader and a person to be feared rather than respected.

The **stark difference** between the commitment demonstrated by Florence Nightingale and her **devotion to serving others** and the **questionable conduct** of this university leader reinforces the fact that **feminine leadership and its qualities are not automatically associated with gender.**

♀♂

Feminine Leadership Not Perfectly Correlated By Gender

After this woman's brother stepped down and finally retired as president, this woman retired shortly thereafter – to the relief of many who worked within that university. Although she was a female in a leadership role, this individual lacked the caring consideration for others – beyond a select few of her closest associates. She was viewed by many individuals as a leader who was lacking in a moral perspective and a person who failed to honor the high ideals and values of the university where she was employed – which happened to be a church-owned academic institution.

The stark difference between the commitment demonstrated by Florence Nightingale and her devotion to serving others and the questionable conduct of this university leader reinforces the fact that feminine leadership and its qualities are not automatically associated with gender. Feminine leadership skills are clearly more likely to be associated with females with males, but the evidence is nonetheless clear that gender and the effective utilization of engaging others, demonstrating commitment to their welfare, and honoring responsibilities associated with relationships are not always adopted by leaders – even when those qualities can greatly increase the effectiveness of organizations.

Florence Nightingale sought to **do no harm to others.** Her negative counterpart left **pain, devastation, and shattered lives** in her wake.

In the case of the university leader, her personal leadership style seemed to lack basic consideration for others, a clear sense of ethical and moral perspective, and the inability to recognize that her role was to inspire and serve others – rather than to attempt to dominate and control them. Florence Nightingale sought to do no harm to others. Her negative counterpart left pain, devastation, and shattered lives in her wake.

SIX INSIGHTS FOR LEADERS

Feminine Leadership has the potential to make a profound difference in the lives of those whom leaders serve, as well as in the organizations where leaders who adopt its principles work[292].

---

[292] Chemers, M., (2014), *op. cit.* and Jironet, K., (2019), *op. cit.* These six insights that follow incorporate the perspectives of both sources.

1. Feminine Leadership Increases Commitment by Demonstrating Greater Concern for Employees' Welfare

The feminine leadership perspective emphasizes responsibilities owed to each individual employee and reflects a more personal commitment to others' welfare. The feminine leader's commitment to others honors the moral obligations of leadership that are often not fulfilled by other leaders[293].

2. Feminine Leadership's Commitment to Honoring Relationship-Based Duties and Obligations Generates Greater Employee Trust

Feminine leadership's commitment to caring relationships is a fundamental element that characterizes those who adopt it. By demonstrating this commitment to all of the members of the organization and by incorporating the Ethic of Care, leaders who employee the feminine leadership perspective demonstrate that they are worthy of employees' trust.

---

[293] The leader's moral obligations to others are identified throughout DePree, M., (2004). *Leadership is an Art*. New York: Crown Publishing.

By demonstrating this commitment to all of the members of the organization and **by incorporating the Ethic of Care**, leaders who employee the feminine leadership perspective **demonstrate that they are worthy of employees' trust.**

3. Feminine Leadership Generates Increased Employee Creativity by a Communicating Style That Is more Participative and Focused on Listening Rather Than Telling

By their interactive communication style and their willingness to listen to employees' suggestions, leaders who demonstrate a feminine leadership perspective are able to generate greater employee involvement and ownership in the creative process. Creativity and innovation are important for constant improvement.

Leaders who demonstrate a feminine leadership perspective are **able to generate greater employee involvement and ownership** in the creative process. **Creativity and innovation** are important for **constant improvement.**

4. Feminine Leadership Acknowledges the Need for Greater Employee Work Life Balance Which Reduces Employee Stress and Burnout

Although leaders with a feminine leadership perspective are committed to achieving an organization's purpose and goals, they recognize that those goals are dependent upon an appropriate work life balance. By acknowledging and supporting that balance, they enhance the long-term sustainability of organizations.

Although leaders with a feminine leadership perspective are committed to achieving **an organization's purpose and goals**, they recognize that those goals are **dependent upon an appropriate work life balance.**

5. Feminine Leadership Views the Work Context in a More Holistic Way and Is Thereby Able to Maintain a Clearer Perspective about Priorities

Demonstrating commitment to **the success of employees *and* the organization,** helps to **create greater synergy** in pursuing goals that **benefit** both.

By recognizing the value of the individual as well as the organization, leaders with a feminine leadership perspective incorporate a greater transformational perspective. Demonstrating commitment to the success of employees *and* the organization, helps to create greater synergy in pursuing goals that benefit both.

6. Feminine Leadership Emphasizes Teamwork Rather Than Individual Contributions Which Enables Organizations to Be More Collaborative in the Pursuit of Organizational Goals

The feminine leadership perspective seeks cooperation and recognizes that the achievement of high standards is best accomplished by joint efforts rather than by people working singly. Cooperation and teamwork enhance employee ownership.

The feminine leadership perspective **seeks cooperation** and recognizes that the **achievement of high standards** is best accomplished **by joint efforts** rather than by people working singly.

Each of these six insights has great practical value in organizations that struggle to earn the trust of employees and to utilize their talents to compete in the global marketplace.

CONCLUSION

In a world that is increasingly challenged by problems that demand increased cooperation and greater innovation, there is much value in the contributions that are available from the feminine leadership perspective[294]. Today's employees, particularly younger employees who view work as a means for achieving their own personal objectives, require a leadership style that demonstrates a commitment to their individual interests as well as the needs of the organization where those employees work.

Today's employees, particularly **younger employees who view work as a means for achieving their own personal objectives,** require a **leadership style that demonstrates a commitment to their individual interests** as well as the needs of the organization where those employees work.

Incorporating a leadership perspective that **demonstrates authentic caring** and that **empower employees** makes it possible for the modern organization to **unlock the potential** of employees that is **so often underutilized.**

[294] *Ibid.*

The feminine leadership perspective provides organizations with a means for utilizing the creativity and the potential that is often overlooked by traditional high control, high compliance leadership perspectives. Incorporating a leadership perspective that demonstrates authentic caring and that empower employees makes it possible for the modern organization to unlock the potential of employees that is so often underutilized.

As a model of deeply committed and highly effective feminine leadership, Florence Nightingale's example of servant leadership and personal dedication is an inspiring model for other leaders – both men and women – to follow. By incorporating the strengths of feminine leadership and recognizing its benefits, those who lead can add value to their organizations while demonstrating feminine leadership's moral commitment to the best interests of employees as well. As leaders serve others and apply the principles of feminine leadership, they honor their individual callings and fulfill a noble purpose that enriches others' lives.

As leaders **serve others** and **apply the principles** of feminine leadership, they **honor their individual callings** and fulfill a noble purpose that **enriches others' lives.**

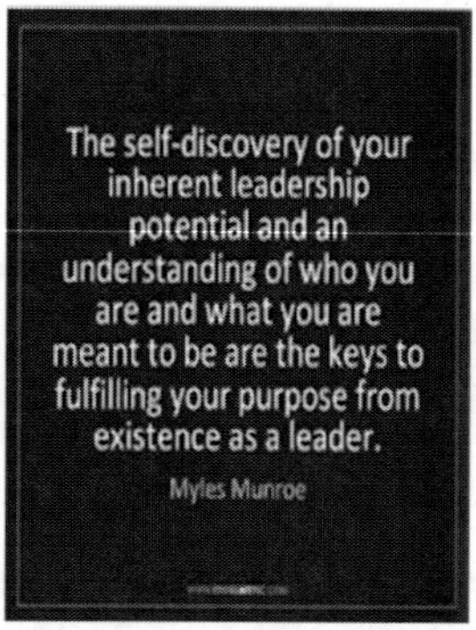

Chapter 8

LEADERSHIP AND RESPONSIBILITY

Over the past four decades, one of the major issues confronting organizations and their leaders has been "What is the extent of our responsibilities, beyond our financial duty to our shareholders?" This question about the scope of a leader's role has spurred a vigorous debate about core principles of organizational governance that challenged basic assumptions about economic theory, moral philosophy, and the obligations of the corporation.

Over the past four decades, one of the major issues confronting organizations and their leaders has been "What is the extent of our responsibilities, beyond our financial duty to our shareholders?" This question about the scope of a leader's role has spurred a vigorous debate about core principles of organizational governance that challenged basic assumptions about economic theory, moral philosophy, and the obligations of the corporation.

The purpose of this chapter is to address the importance of social responsibility as a leadership obligation. The chapter begins by briefly summarizing five theories of organizational governance and distinguishing their varying perspectives about the leader's role. After providing this overview, the chapter then describes the actions of two different leaders.

One of those leaders is Muhammud Yunus, a social entrepreneur and the founder of the Grameen Bank who was ultimately awarded the Nobel Prize for his service to others. The other leader was Chief Executive Officer of one of the world's most successful corporations whose company polluted a major U.S. river and who served at the company's helm while it delayed the clean-up of that river for two decades. The chapter concludes with four recommendations for leaders regarding their role in guiding the social responsibility of their companies.

GOVERNANCE AND THE LEADER'S ROLE

Governance of organizations is the process by which (1) an organization is managed to optimize performance and accountability, (2) its values are reflected by the systems and structures that are created, (3) relationships are established that create the commitment of those who work within the organization, and (4) leadership is formally applied as the purpose of an organization is achieved[295]. There are five established models of organizational governance, with each model based upon a theory of governance.

Table 1 briefly provides a brief summary of the five governance models, the leader's purpose and primary commitment, and a comment about the leader's role.

---

[295] Caldwell, C., and Hansen, M., (2010). "Trustworthiness, Governance, and Wealth Creation." *Journal of Business Ethics*, Vol. 97, Iss. 2, pp. 173-188.

Governance of organizations is the process by which (1) an organization is managed to optimize performance and accountability, (2) its values are reflected by the systems and structures that are created, (3) relationships are established that create the commitment of those who work within the organization, and (4) leadership is formally applied as the purpose of an organization is achieved.

Table 1. Leader roles, purpose and commitment in governance models

Governance Model	Summary of Theory	Leadership Purpose	Primary Commitment	Comment
Agency Theory	The leader is a hired professional to provide competent leadership to benefit shareholders.	Provide competent guidance to achieve shareholder profits as directed.	Serves shareholders who provide financial incentives.	Agent may pursue strategies that benefit her/his self-interest.
Stakeholder Theory	The leader is hired to benefit the needs of all the stakeholders.	Identify benefits that satisfy different stake-holder priorities.	Balance divergent needs through compromise.	The agent's focus is on "satisficing" to meet others' needs.
Stewardship Theory	The leader is hired to optimize long-term wealth creation.	Provide guidance and develop all stakeholders to achieve best outcome.	Serve as a moral compass to benefit all long-term.	Must fiercely model values to be perceived as credible.
Principle Theory	Leader is hired to guide organization according to defined principles.	Ensure that the values and principles espoused are followed by all parties.	Commitment is to the philosophy and principles of the organization.	The organization's principles sometimes affect sustainability of the organization.
Principal Theory	Leader is entirely subservient to the principals or shareholders.	Comply with shareholder directives and achieve their goals.	Totally dependent upon the shareholders and meeting their needs.	Needs of other stakeholders are viewed as transactional.

For each of these five governance models, the leader's purpose and primary commitment affects his or her role and sense of moral responsibility to the shareholders, other stakeholders, and society. For the leader serving the organization within the Agency, Principle, and Principal Theory models, the primary role of the leader is in serving the needs of the shareholders and acting under their direction to achieve their goals.

For each of these five governance models, **the leader's purpose and primary commitment affects his or her role** and sense of **moral responsibility** to the shareholders, other stakeholders, and society.

Under the Stakeholder Theory model, the leader is an accommodator of the conflicting desires of the many stakeholders of the firm –compromising long-term outcomes for short-term desires. It is within the context of Stewardship Theory that the leader seeks to optimize long-term value creation that benefits the organization over time and that honors moral duties owed to the stakeholders and society.

It is within the context of **Stewardship Theory** that the leader seeks to **optimize long-term value creation** that benefits the organization over time and that **honors moral duties** owed to the stakeholders and society.

Social Responsibility Perspectives

Social responsibility acknowledges that individuals and organizations have a moral obligation to act in the best interests of society, as well as benefiting their internal organizational stakeholders[296]. This obligation complies with the obligations of moral intelligence to 1) do no harm, 2) create value in the short-term, and 3) create value in the long-term[297]. By so doing, an organization serves its customers and creates profits for shareholders while honoring duties to their employees and to society at large.

Social responsibility acknowledges that individuals and organizations have **a moral obligation to act in the best interests of society**, as well as benefiting their internal organizational stakeholders. This obligation complies with the obligations of moral intelligence to 1) **do no harm**, 2) **create value in the short-term**, and 3) **create value in the long-term**.

Ethicists and scholars have argued extensively about the complex set of economic, political, and moral duties owed by businesses to their shareholders[298]. From the days of Adam Smith, the perspective of many business leaders has focused on an ethical perspective of the pursuit of

---

[296] Anderson, V., Ndalamba, K. K., and Caldwell, C., (2017). "Social Responsibility in a Troubled World: A Virtuous Perspective." *International Journal of Public Leadership*, Vol, 13, Iss. 2, pp 98-115.

[297] These three requirements of moral responsibility are identified in Lennick, D. & Kiel, F., (2011). *Moral Intelligence 2.0: Enhancing Business Performance and Leadership Success in Turbulent Times*. Upper Saddle River, NJ: FT Press.

[298] Anderson, V., Ndalamba, K. K., and Caldwell, C., (2017), *op. cit.*

individual self-interest[299]. The economic principle of "the invisible hand" that Smith espoused argued that the pursuit of individual self-interests would ultimately benefit society in the long-term by influencing supply and demand[300]. Smith's ideas dominated economic principles of free market capitalism for the better part of two centuries, and were reaffirmed by a 1970 article by the Nobel Prize winning economist, Milton Friedman[301].

> The economic principle of "the invisible hand" that Smith espoused argued that **the pursuit of individual self-interests would ultimately benefit society** in the long-term by influencing supply and demand. Smith's ideas **dominated economic principles of free market capitalism** for the better part of two centuries, and were **reaffirmed by a 1970 article by the Nobel Prize winning economist, Milton Friedman.**

Friedman argued that the role of the agent was purely to serve the needs of its organization's shareholders.

> In a free-enterprise, private-property system, a corporate executive is an employee of the owners of the business. He has direct responsibility to his employers. That responsibility is to conduct the business in accordance with their desires, which generally will be to make as much money as possible while conforming to their basic rules of the society, both those embodied in law and those embodied in ethical custom. Of course, in some cases his employers may have a different objective. A group of persons might establish a corporation for an eleemosynary purpose – for example,

[299] See Smith, A., (1759). *The Theory of Moral Sentiments*. London and Edinburgh, UK: A. Strahan; and T. Cadell, in the Strand; and T. Creech and J. Bell & Co. at Edinburgh.

[300] *Ibid.*

[301] This famous and frequently-quoted article by Friedman is found at Friedman, M., (1970). "The Social Responsibility of Business is to Increase its Profits." *New York Times Magazine*. Found online on December 30, 2019 at http://www.umich.edu/~thecore/doc/Friedman.pdf.

> a hospital or a school. The manager of such a corporation will not have money profit as his objectives but the rendering of certain services.

This perspective essentially summarized the Agency Theory of governance. Friedman argued that for an agent leader to divert shareholder revenues for a social purpose was to unnecessarily increase the costs of goods and services to customers while violating the obligation of the leader to the investors in the organization[302].

From a practical historical perspective, the evidence suggests that **Friedman's ideals have proven to be unrealistic.** Not only do laws and customs vary markedly throughout different parts of the world, but 1) individual shareholders and shareholder groups have **lobbied to create laws that benefit them at the expense of society,** and 2) **governments and legal systems have failed to adequately protect the long-term impact of businesses** on the larger community.

Friedman's perspective assumed, as he noted, that "the basic rules of the society, both those embodied in law and those embodied in ethical custom" would protect society and the common interest[303]. From a practical historical perspective, the evidence suggests that Friedman's ideals have proven to be unrealistic. Not only do laws and customs vary markedly throughout different parts of the world, but 1) individual shareholders and shareholder groups have lobbied to create laws that benefit them at the expense of society, and 2) governments and legal systems have failed to adequately protect the long-term impact of businesses on the larger community[304].

---

[302] *Ibid.*

[303] *Ibid.*

[304] The reality of these negative impacts has been broadly documented in a multitude of sources. See, for example, Friedman, T. L., (2009), *op. cit.*

The counterbalancing position to the Adam Smith-Milton Friedman argument about the obligations of business has nevertheless been well established. From the time of the Greek city-states, those who governed recognized that the public good needed to be protected by both judicious oversight and clear moral expectations[305]. Merchants were granted the right to do business only if they could demonstrate that they could make a positive contribution that would benefit society[306]. Aristotelian virtue ethics required that individuals and organizations created value without doing harm to others[307].

From the time of the Greek city-states, **those who governed recognized that the public good needed to be protected** by both **judicious oversight** and **clear moral expectations.** Merchants were granted the right to do business **only if they could demonstrate that they could make a positive contribution** that would benefit society.

RESPONSIBLE BUSINESS

The current corporate social responsibility position affirms the needs of all stakeholders to work cooperatively to create value that benefits the firm and the entire community[308]. This perspective argues that an organization's responsibility goes beyond wealth creation and requires that a company contribute corporate citizenship benefits as a fundamental moral obligation

---

[305] Manville, B. & Ober, J., (2003). *A Company of Citizens: What the World's First Democracy Teaches Leaders About Creating Great Organizations*. Boston, MA: Harvard Business Review Press.

[306] *Ibid.*

[307] This important obligation of business is explained in great detail in Solomon, R. C., (1992). *Ethics and Excellence: Cooperation and Integrity in Business*.

[308] Freeman, R. E. (1984). *Strategic Management: A Stakeholder Approach*. New York: Cambridge University Press.

owed to society. Although shareholders deserve a reasonable return on investment, the compelling problems facing the world also demand that businesses share in the responsibility to serve the public good and address the problems which must be faced by tomorrow's generations[309].

Although **shareholders deserve a reasonable return** on investment, the **compelling problems facing the world also demand that businesses share in the responsibility** to serve the public good and **address the problems which must be faced** by tomorrow's generations.

Muhammud Yunus and the Grameen Bank

Muhammud Yunus is a Bengali social entrepreneur who was responsible for creating the Grameen bank. Yunus obtained a PhD from Vanderbilt University in economics and, following the Bangladesh Liberation War in 1971, he returned to his home country and became involved in a poverty reduction program within his country[310]. While visiting households in the village of Jobra, Yunus discovered that very small loans could make a disproportionate difference to poor individuals within that community. Yunus learned that village women who made furniture out of bamboo had to take high interest loans to buy their bamboo[311].

---

309 Friedman, T. L., (2009). *Hot, Flat, and Crowded: Why We Need a Green Revolution – And How It Can Renew America, Release 2.0*. New York: Picador Press.

310 Yunus, M., (2008). *Banker to the Poor: Micro-Lending and the Battle Against World Poverty*. Philadelphia, PA: Perseus Books.

311 *Ibid*,

Muhammud Yunus is a **Bengali social entrepreneur** who was **responsible for creating the Grameen bank.** . . While visiting households in the village of Jobra, Yunus discovered that **very small loans could make a disproportionate difference to poor individuals** within that community.

Muhammud Yunus

Traditional banks in Bangladesh were unwilling to make small loans at a reasonable interest to the poor due to their belief that the borrowers constituted a high risk of default. Yunus believed that, given the chance, the borrowers would repay the money and was convinced that a microcredit was a viable business opportunity. Lending only $27 of his money to 42 women in the village, Yunus made a profit of two cents on each on the 42 loans[312].

Beginning in 1976, Yunus secured a loan from the government Janata Bank to finance loans to the poor in Jobra. Building on that success, Yunus secured additional loans from other banks for microloan projects. By 1982, Yunus' pilot project had generated 28,000 members and by 1983, the pilot project began operation as Grameen Bank.

Despite opposition from opponents as diverse as violent radical leftists and conservative Muslim clergy, Yunus' simple idea had grown to $6.38 billion in loans offered to 7.4 million borrowers. Other microcredit loan projects adopted the Grameen Bank model – growing to serve the poor in 100 developing countries and even in the United States[313]. Yunus received the Nobel Prize in recognition of his work fighting poverty in 2006[314].

---

[312]Yunus, M. (2011). *Building Social Business: The New Kind of Capitalism that Serves Humanity's Most Pressing Needs*. Philadelphia, PA: Perseus Books.

[313] "Grameen Bank Facts." (2006). *NobelPrize.org*. Found online on December 30, 2019 at https://www.nobelprize.org/prizes/peace/2006/grameen/facts/.

[314] *Ibid.*

Despite opposition from opponents as diverse as violent radical leftists and conservative Muslim clergy, Yunus' simple idea had grown to $6.38 billion in loans offered to 7.4 million borrowers. Other microcredit loan projects adopted the Grameen Bank model – growing to serve the poor in 100 developing countries and even in the United States. Yunus received the Nobel Prize in recognition of his work fighting poverty in 2006.

THE POLLUTING GIANT

In contrast with Muhammud Yunus, a Chief Executive Officer (CEO) of a major U.S. corporation stalled, delayed, and orchestrated to avoid cleaning up the pollution of one of America's most noted rivers – pollution that his company acknowledged that it was responsible for causing for more than five decades. From 1947 to 1977, the company polluted a major U.S. river by discharging 1.3 million pounds of polychlorinated biphenyls (PCBs), causing a broad range of harmful effects to wildlife as well as the people who eat fish or drink the water from the river. PCBs are known to be toxic agents which disrupt the endocrine function and negatively affect the central and peripheral nervous systems[315].

[315] Ritchie, G. D., Still, K. R., Alexander, W. K.; Nordholm, A. F,; Wilson, C. L.,Rossi, J., & Mattie, D. R. (2001). "A Review of the Neurotoxicity Risk of selected Hydrocarbon Fuels". *Journal of Toxicology and Environmental Health. Part B, Critical Reviews*, Volume 4, No. 3, pp.: 223–312.

From 1947 to 1977, the company **polluted a major U.S. river by discharging 1.3.million pounds of polychlorinated biphenyls** (PCBs), causing a broad range of **harmful effects to wildlife as well as the people who eat fish or drink the water** from the river.

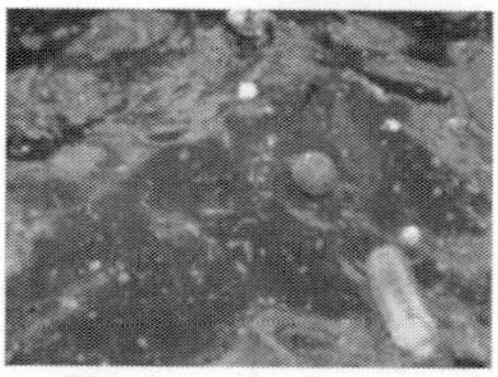

Remarkably, **the long-time corporate CEO, who had fought the river cleanup** from the time of his inauguration in 1981 to his retirement in 2001, **declared to the world that "PCBs are safe" – despite clear scientific evidence** to the contrary.

Despite the fact that the dangers of PCBs were well established in the 1960s, the company continued to pollute in full knowledge of the associated risks to wildlife and to the public. Worse yet, under the leadership of its CEO, the company was able to stall, delay, and otherwise put off the remediation of its pollution of this major tributary to 2009 – when it was finally ordered by the Environmental Protection Agency (EPA) to clean up 2,650,000 cubic yards of sediment in the river. Remarkably, the long-time corporate CEO, who had fought the river cleanup from the time of his inauguration in 1981 to his retirement in 2001, declared to the world that "PCBs are safe" – despite clear scientific evidence to the contrary.

Although the EPA finally granted the company a "Certificate of Completion" for the project – after ten years – the state's Department of Environmental Conservation continues to consider the clean-up project inadequate and has declared the river "unacceptably contaminated." During the time that the CEO headed the company, its net worth increased 4000% – but the CEO fought spending the money to clean up the river for his entire tenure in office – and he retired with a severance payment of over $400 million for his efforts.

During the time that the CEO headed the company, its **net worth increased 4000%** -- but the CEO **fought spending the money to clean up the river for his entire tenure** in office – and he retired with a **severance payment of over $400 million for his efforts.**

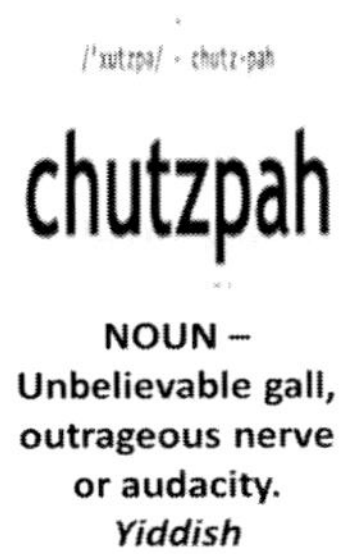

The stark contrast in the examples of these two individuals in their attitude toward social responsibility is glaring. In one case, Muhammud Yunus made the effort to literally change the world for millions of individuals and their families who endured third-world poverty. In the other case, the CEO of a major corporation used every imaginable device at his access to avoid honoring a responsibility for which his company was clearly to blame that threatened both the environment and the health of literally millions of his state's residents.

In one case, Muhammud Yunus **made the effort to literally change the world for millions of individuals** and their families who endured third-world poverty. In the other case, the CEO of a major corporation **used every imaginable device at his access to avoid honoring a responsibility for which his company was clearly to blame** that threatened both the environment and the health of literally millions of his state's residents.

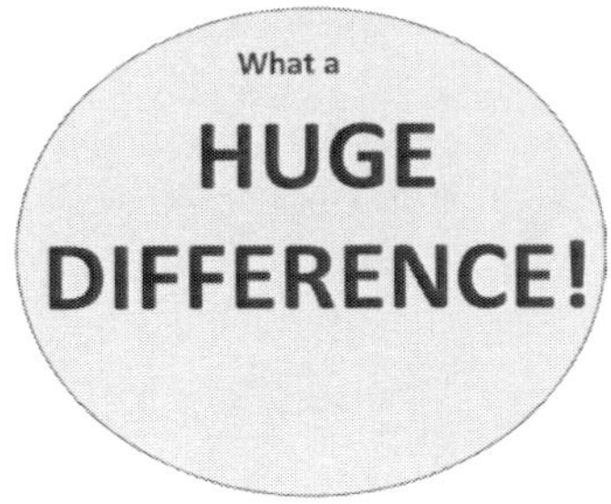

FOUR SOCIAL RESPONSIBILITY RECOMMENDATIONS

As leaders reflect on their own obligations to be socially responsible, as well as the obligations of the organizations for which they labor, they can improve their own personal credibility and that of their companies by considering four specific recommendations.

1. Examine and Reaffirm Your Own Personal Values

Unfortunately, it is not uncommon for personal values to be overlooked when organizations and leaders find themselves under pressure to achieve a major goal or to meet a critical deadline. Being committed to a fixed set of absolute principles and values is a vital step to ensuring that one's conduct adheres to those ideals. It is far too easy to put off being committed to moral and ethical principles by simply avoiding articulating them[316]. For a leader, and for the people (s)he serves, defining those personal values and principles sends an important message to the organization about what is important. In addition, formally acknowledging those values to oneself improves the likelihood that those values will be followed.

Being committed to a fixed set of absolute principles and values is a vital step to ensuring that one's conduct adheres to those ideals. It is far too easy to put off being committed to moral and ethical principles by simply avoiding articulating them.

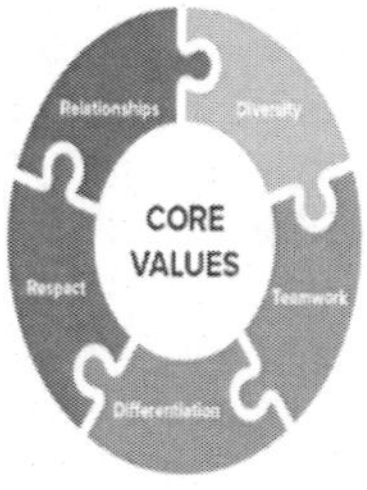

[316] This vital point is identified in Christensen, C. M., Allworth, J. & Dillon, K. (2012). *How Will You Measure Your Life?* New York: HarperCollins.

2. Determine Your Stakeholders and the Duties Owed to Them

In the hurly-burly of day-to-day activities and monumental responsibilities, it is sometimes convenient for leaders to find short-cuts and quick fix solutions attractive. However, those temporary solutions and "just this once" accommodations set the tone to others about duties owed[317]. Formally addressing the duties owed to stakeholders – not just to shareholders and investors but to all an organization's stakeholders – is a necessary task to avoid a misstep that can discredit an organization and destroy a leader's reputation. Thinking hard about the long-term implications of duties owed to stakeholders, including those obligations owed to future generations, can protect both the reputation of an organization and the personal credibility of its leaders.

Thinking hard about the long-term implications of duties owed to stakeholders, including those obligations owed to future generations, can protect both the reputation of an organization and the personal credibility of its leaders.

3. Identify Opportunities to Add Value Short-Term and Long-Term

Trading a short-term benefit for a significant long-term cost often results in the inability of organizations to compete successfully. The steward's focus on long-term benefits and the creation of value is a perspective that is most often the best decision and that earns the trust and respect of others

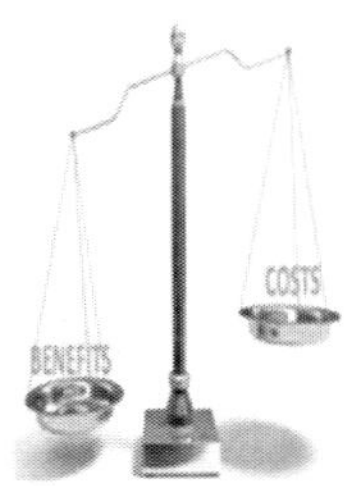

317 *Ibid.*

Recognizing the long-term goals of an organization can be critical to enabling an organization to avoid a critical short-term blunder. Both short-term and long-term outcomes are part of each leader's set of moral obligations. Trading a short-term benefit for a significant long-term cost often results in the inability of organizations to compete successfully[318]. The steward's focus on long-term benefits and the creation of value is a perspective that is most often the best decision and that earns the trust and respect of others.

4. Compare Your Performance with the Values You Espouse

Values that exist on paper but that are not applied in day-to-day decisions serve to erode trust, undermine employee commitment, and demonstrate that a leader is not only untrustworthy but also dishonest. When leaders do what they say they will do, they send a powerful message to their customers, their employees, their peers, and their shareholders that they deserve the positions of responsibility that they hold[319].

Each of these four recommendations is a useful touchstone for leaders to incorporate as they assess their own decisions, the choices made by the

[318] Caldwell, C. & Hansen, M., (2010), *op. cit.*

[319] Kouzes, J. M. & Posner, B. Z., (2017). The Leadership Challenge: How to Make Extraordinary Things Happen in Organizations (6th ed.). San Francisco, CA: Jossey-Bass.

people with whom they work, and the consequences of their organization's impact on the world. Organizations must also be financially responsible and leaders play an important role in being efficient, profitable, and effective at accomplishing their primary purpose. Despite those realities, financial success is not enough and leaders also have an obligation to be socially responsible in honoring duties owed to all of their stakeholders – including those of future generations.

Organizations **must also be financially responsible** and leaders play an important role in being efficient, profitable, and effective at accomplishing their primary purpose. Despite those realities, **financial success is not enough and leaders also have an obligation to be socially responsible** in honoring duties owed to **all of their stakeholders – including those of future generations.**

A Challenge to Leaders

Being accountable to high standards enables leaders to be perceived as honorable and trustworthy – but being accountable requires knowing one's own identity and the values that guide one's life. As leaders examine their own philosophy of governance, the ideals of the ethical steward are clearly standards which leaders recognize to be in the interests of the many stakeholders that they serve.

As leaders examine their own philosophy of governance, **the ideals of the ethical steward** are clearly standards which leaders recognize to be **in the interests of the many stakeholders** that they serve.

Social responsibility requires that a leader is willing to commit herself or himself to principles, values, and practices that honor obligations and duties owed to others. Although short-term self-interest may seem to be an attractive choice from time to time, the cost of many short-term gains can also equate to a loss of personal integrity and, ultimately, the loss of credibility for a leader and his or her organization.

Although short-term self-interest **may seem to be an attractive choice** from time to time, the cost of many **short-term gains can also equate to a loss of personal integrity and, ultimately, the loss of credibility** for a leader and his or her organization.

The two powerful examples of Muhammud Yunus and the CEO of the company that polluted a major U.S. river are profound testaments to the wide difference in moral responsibility and personal integrity that leaders can demonstrate. As leaders reflect upon those two examples, it is absolutely clear that the action of Muhammud Yunus were both incredibly intelligent and socially significant . . . just as it is also clear that the choices made by the CEO were self-serving, detrimental, and socially irresponsible.

Choosing the moral high ground and the path that honors relationships, that adds value to stakeholders, and that serves society long-term ultimately is a choice that garners others' respect and trust – and that enables organizations and leaders to be part of the solutions necessary to create a better world for future generations. As leaders demonstrate social responsibility in their personal choices and in their relationships with stakeholders, they define themselves and their organizations and confirm their own personal value as well as the value of their companies.

As leaders **demonstrate social responsibility** in their **personal choices** and in their **relationships with stakeholders**, they **define themselves** and their organizations and **confirm their own personal value** as well as the **value of their companies.**

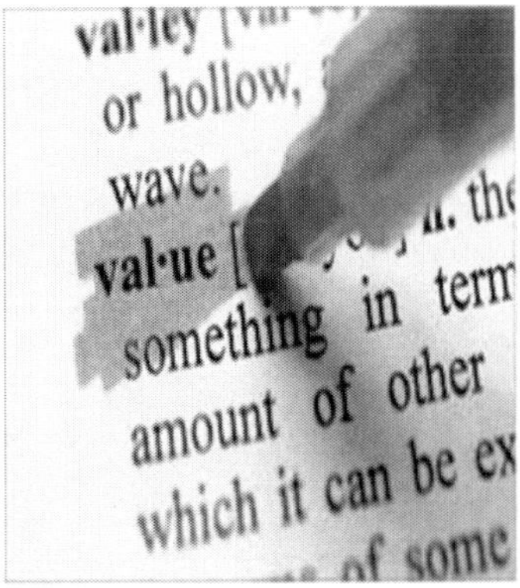

Chapter 9

LEADERS DEVELOP PEOPLE: SERVICE AT THE PERSONAL LEVEL

Regardless of how personally competent, committed, and credible a leader may be, that leader is **not going to be optimally effective** if (s)he **does not develop others** and help them **to become their very best version** of themselves.

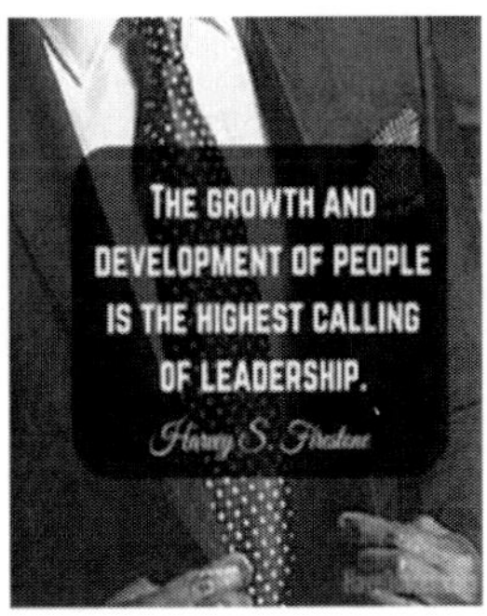

Regardless of how personally competent, committed, and credible a leader may be, that leader is not going to be optimally effective if (s)he does not develop others and help them to become their very best version of themselves[320]. It is ultimately by creating an organization of top performers who work together effectively that leaders are most effective in competing in the international arena. Great leaders not only constantly seek to improve themselves but they are also deeply committed to developing others.

---

[320] This principle is well documented by many leadership scholars. See, for example, the extensive research of Stephen R. Covey. Warren G. Bennis, and James McGregor Burns.

The focus of this chapter is on the vital role of leaders in serving others, developing others' capacity as leaders themselves, and utilizing those skills to effectively benefit their organizations. The chapter begins by identifying seven important ways in which effective leaders are able to develop the abilities of those with whom they work. Following that introduction, the chapter contrasts the success of Max DePree, former Chief Executive Officer of Herman Miller Furniture, with the ineffective outcomes of a school administrator who treated his staff and faculty like commodities and ended up achieving far less for his college and his students than that which was potentially achievable.

Leaders play a vital role by **serving others, developing their capacities** as leaders, and **utilizing those skills** to effectively **benefit their organizations.**

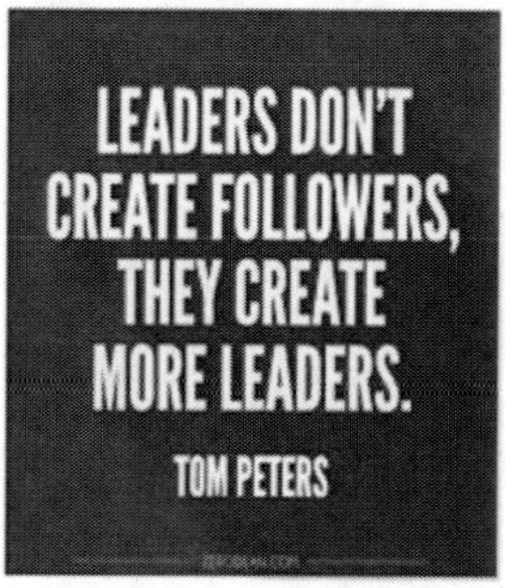

The chapter then identifies six important principles about the leader's role in developing others and identifies the benefits achieved for leaders who incorporate those principles in their personal leadership approach. The chapter concludes with a challenge to leaders to honor their obligation to help others to develop their individual capabilities – both to benefit themselves and their organizations and to create added value within their communities.

DEVELOPING OTHERS

The obligation of leaders to be committed to the best interests of others – and, particularly, to the employees with whom they work – has been a recurring theme that has been addressed in moral philosophy, leadership ethics, and theories of governance. LaRue Hosmer wrote extensively about the correlation between organizational theory and philosophical ethics and noted that leaders earned trust by honoring duties owed to employees[321].

The obligation of leaders to be **committed to the best interests of others** – and, particularly, **to the employees with whom they work** – has been a **recurring theme** that has been **addressed in moral philosophy, leadership ethics, and theories of governance.**

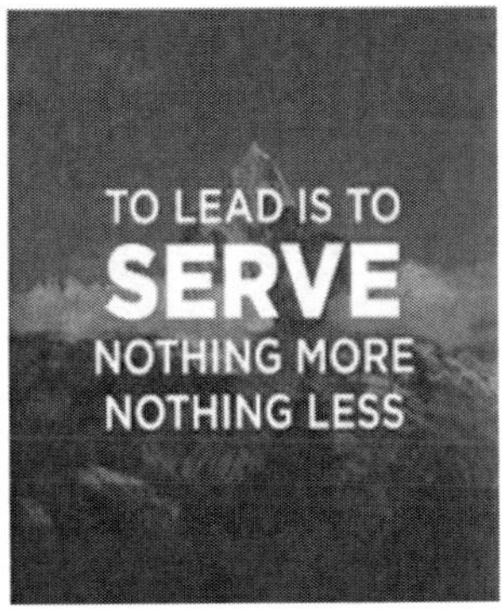

Other scholars have also written about the obligation of leaders in demonstrating a commitment to the welfare and best interests of employees, describing that duty as a transformational responsibility that benefited the organization as well as its employees[322]. Servant leadership[323], authentic leadership[324], and transformative leadership[325] theories all address the obligations of leaders in developing others and in working for their best interests. In examining the nature of the leader's responsibilities to develop their employees, there are seven important ways that leaders can fulfill this commitment.

---

321 Hosmer, L. T., (1995). "Trust: The Connecting Link between Organizational Theory and Philosophical Ethics." *Academy of Management Review*, Vol. 20, No. 2, pp. 379-403.

322 See, for example, the work of Burns and his discussion of transformational leadership in., J. M., (2010). *Leadership*. New York: Harper Perennial.

323 Greenleaf, R. K. & Spears, L. C., (2002). *Servant Leadership: A Journey into the Nature of Legitimate Power and Greatness 25th Anniversary Edition*. Mahwah, NJ: Paulist Press.

324 George, B., (2004). *Authentic Leadership: Rediscovering the Secrets to Creating Lasting Value*. San Francisco, CA: Jossey-Bass.

325 Caldwell, C., (2012). *Moral Leadership: A Transformative Model for Tomorrow's Leaders*. New York: Business Expert Press.

1. Kind and Supportive Caring

Although many practitioners and academics have described leadership as an "arms-length" relationship[326], others view the leader's role as much more personal. The obligation to "lead with love" has been conveyed by leaders in virtually all work contexts – including settings as diverse as the military and the shop floor[327]. Perhaps the clearest summary of the leader's responsibility to care for employees is Stephen R. Covey's definition of leadership as treating employees so well that they come to recognize their greatness and strive to achieve it[328].

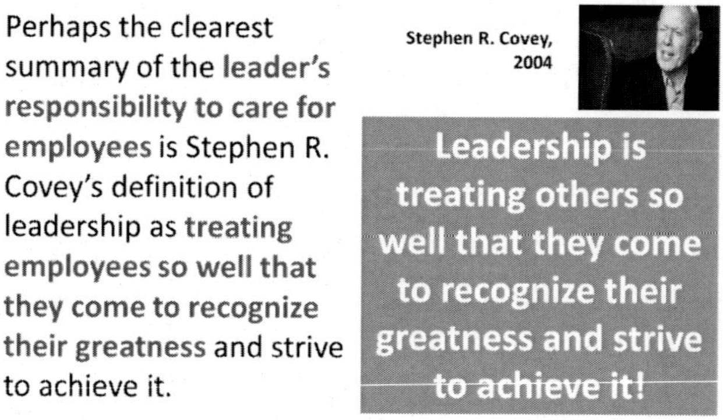

2. Empowerment and Opportunity

Empowerment of others and providing them with the opportunity to exercise responsibility related to their organizational roles not only gives individuals self-determination but expands their potential to contribute to

[326] Anderson, V., Caldwell, C., & Barfuss, B. (2019). "Love: The Heart of Leadership." *Graziadio Business Review,* Vol. 22, Iss. 2 and may be found online at https://gbr.pepperdine.edu/2019/08/love-the-heart-of-leadership/

[327] See, for example, Caldwell, C., and Dixon, R. D. (2010). "Love, Forgiveness, and Trust: Critical Values of the Modern Leader." *Journal of Business Ethics*, Vol. 93, Iss. 1, pp. 91-101.

[328] The importance of this definition of leadership and the leader's obligation to help others to "find their voice" is the primary theme in Covey, S. R., (2004). *The 8th Habit: From Effectiveness to Greatness*. New York: Free Press, p. 98.

organizational goal achievement[329]. Leaders who empower their employees enable them to have the learning experiences that enable them to enhance their performance. The trust demonstrated by the leader who delegates and empowers allows employees to grow and to become more valuable contributors to an organization[330].

The trust demonstrated by **the leader who delegates and empowers** allows employees to **grow and to become more valuable** contributors to an organization.

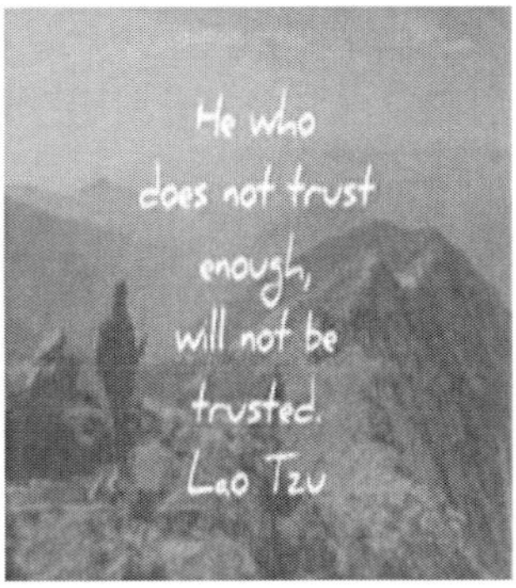

3. Coaching and Supervision

The performance improvement process can be a means of either enhancing and facilitating individual performance or creating negative employee feelings about the organization and about her or his relationship with a supervisor[331]. In contrast with many typical performance appraisal systems, a coaching and mentoring model that supports, encourages, and assists employees to achieve their goals is far superior[332]. Truly effective supervisors strive to assist employees to develop and grow – and organizations that train supervisors in how to coach and mentor are acknowledged to build stronger employee-supervisor relationships.

---

[329] Backlund, S., Backlund, P. & Amato, M. (Eds.) (2016). *The Culture of Empowerment: How to Champion People*. Redding, CA: Igniting Hope Ministries.

[330] *Ibid*.

[331] The potential negative impacts of performance appraisal systems have been addressed by Deming, W. E., (2000). *Out of the Crisis*. Cambridge, MA: MIT Press.

[332] Whitmore, J., (2017). *Coaching for Improved Performance: The Principles and Practices of Coaching and Leadership* (5th ed.). Boston, MA: Nicholas Brealey Publishing.

In contrast with many typical performance appraisal systems, a **coaching and mentoring model** that **supports, encourages, and assists** employees to achieve their goals is **far superior.**

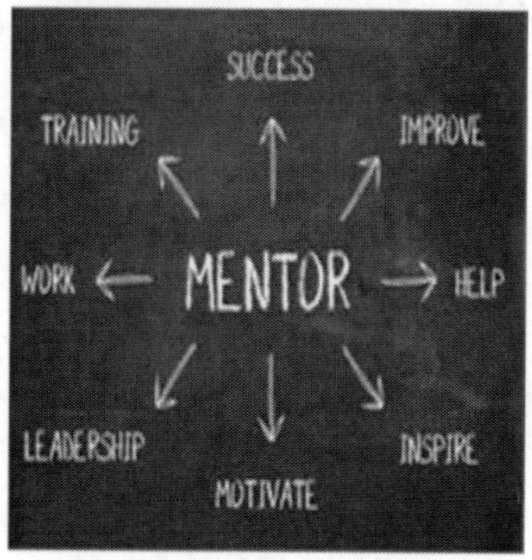

4. Training and Development

Training programs focused on improving employee skills are directly related to employee effectiveness on the job. Organization development training, leadership and management improvement, and communication skills are professional development opportunities that can greatly enhance employee effectiveness in current assignments – as well as preparing employees for future leadership opportunities[333].

Organization development training, leadership and management improvement, and communication skills are **professional development opportunities** that can greatly enhance employee effectiveness in **current assignments** -- as well as preparing employees for **future leadership** opportunities.

---

[333] See Caldwell, C. and Anderson, V., (Eds.). (2018). *Human Resource Management: A Transformative Perspective*. Hauppage, New York: NOVA Publishing.

5. Engagement and Partnership

Employee engagement is an emotional commitment reflecting the degree to which an employee is committed to giving his or her best efforts at work[334]. Employee engagement reflects the degree of relative satisfaction that an employee feels about his work[335] and is commonly directly related to his relationships with his organizational leaders and supervisors[336]. Leaders that demonstrate a commitment to employee needs and involve them as full partners in decision-making are successful in increasing employee engagement and in providing their employees with opportunities to grow[337].

6. Moral and Ethical Commitment

Leaders who seek to honor "covenantal" duties owed to employees treat those employees as ends rather than as a means to their own self-interests or

[334] This definition reflects the responses of Human Resource Professionals in the Glint research report, "The State of Employee Engagement in 2019." *HR.com*, p. 5-6.

[335] *Ibid*, p. 5.

[336] According to Gallup research the employee's relationship with the manager is the key factor determining his or her commitment to the organization. See Clifton, J. & Harter, J., (2019). *It's the Manager: Gallup Finds the Quality of Managers and Team Leaders Is the Single Biggest Factor in Your Organization's Long-Term Success*. Omaha, NE: Gallup Press.

[337] *Ibid*.

those of the organization[338]. Such leaders view their ethical obligation as helping their employees to excel. They believe that both the individual leader and the organization owe sacred duties to employees that are associated with helping employees to grow and develop[339].

Leaders who seek to honor "covenantal" duties owed to employees treat those employees as ends rather than as a means to their own self-interests or those of the organization.

Leadership is a "covenantal" relationship

7. Honest and Candid Feedback

Leaders do their employees a great service in helping them to develop by providing them with information about how they can perform more effectively and develop their skills. It is not uncommon for individuals to overestimate their abilities and their contribution to an organization[340]. Honest and candid feedback that is accompanied by the resources to improve individual skills can enable employees to increase their effectiveness in adding value to the organization and in becoming more personally capable[341].

---

[338] The covenantal leader is the focus of Pava, M., (2003). *Leading with Meaning: Using Covenantal Leadership to Build a Better Organization*. New York: St. Martin's Press.

[339] This sacred ethical obligation is a fundamental responsibility of leaders and is addressed in DePree, M., (2004). *Leadership is an Art*. New York: Crown Publications.

[340] London, M., (2014). *The Power of Feedback*. New York: Routledge.

[341] *Ibid*.

Honest and candid feedback that is **accompanied by the resources to improve individual skills** can enable employees to **increase their effectiveness in adding value** to the organization and in **becoming more personally capable.**

Each of these seven leadership factors can enable organizations to make a significant contribution to developing employees, improving their job performance, and preparing those individuals for future opportunities.

MAX DEPREE AND EMPLOYEE COMMITMENT

Max DePree and the Herman Miller Corporation (HMC) established a culture of excellence deeply rooted to serving employees – a commitment that enabled the company to be listed as one of *Fortune* magazine's most-admired companies in its industry for 21 of 23 years[342]. DePree's approach to employee relationships translated into an inclusive leadership style that gave employees throughout HMC the opportunity to make their voices known and that combined caring leadership with business success[343].

---

[342] Straczynski, S., (2010). "Herman Miller Named 'Most Admired' Company" *Contract Design Network*, March 8, 2010 and found online on January 1, 2020 at https://www.contractdesign.com/news/main/herman-miller-namedmost-admired-company/.

[343] Nulty, P & Llosa, P., (1992). "The National Business Hall of Fame." *Fortune,* Vol. 125, Issue 6, March 23, 1992.

DePree's approach to employee relationships translated into **an inclusive leadership style** that gave employees the **opportunity to make their voices known** and that **combined caring leadership with business success.**

Max DePree

DePree's leadership philosophy was spelled out in his highly regarded book, *Leadership is an Art*. DePree wrote that "(t)he first responsibility of the leader is to define reality. The last is to say thank you. In between the two, the leader must become a servant and a debtor. That sums up the progress of the artful leader[344]." DePree was deeply committed to the leader's "covenantal" responsibility to serve the best interests of employees and treated his employees as valued partners[345]. He believed that the leader's obligation to optimize the success of the firm came from simultaneously seeking to serve its employees[346].

DePree believed that the **leader's obligation to optimize the success** of the firm came from **simultaneously seeking to serve its employees.**

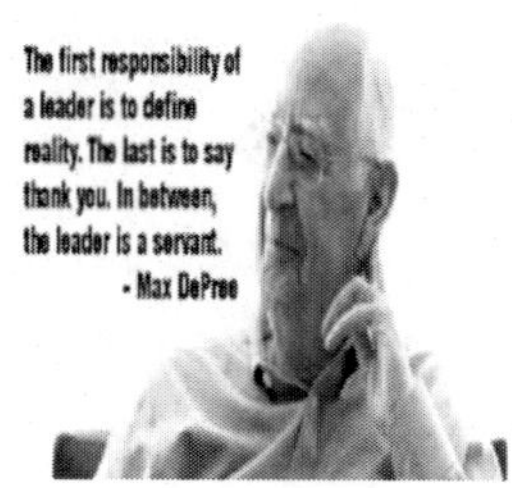

During his forty-year tenure at HMC, Max DePree's commitment to people and the organization helped HMC to be one of the most

---

[344] DePree, M., (2004), *op. cit.*, p. 11.
[345] *Ibid*, Chapter 1.
[346] *Ibid.*

respected companies in the United States[347]. HMC was continually studied for its people-centered leadership style, its unique culture. its constant innovation, the quality of its products, and its excellent return to shareholders[348]. DePree followed the philosophy that the art of leadership lies in "liberating people to do what is required of them in the most effective and humane way possible[349]." DePree personified the servant leader's role of removing obstacles that prevent employees from succeeding at their jobs and helping people to constantly improve[350].

DePree followed the philosophy that **the art of leadership** lies in "**liberating people** to do what is required of them **in the most effective and humane way** possible." DePree **personified the servant leader's role of removing obstacles** that prevent employees from succeeding at their jobs and **helping people to constantly improve.**

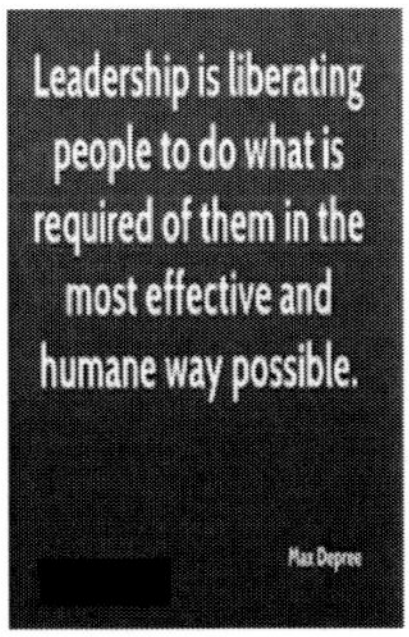

A CONTRASTING EXAMPLE

The chancellor of a small college in a thriving Middle East city is highly trained academically with a PhD. His staff and faculty also consist of competent and committed individuals who have the potential to accomplish great things. Unfortunately, this administrator has failed to take advantage of the skills of his colleagues, has not invested in their personal development, and his chosen instead to direct his college with autocratic fiats.

---

[347] Straczynski, S., (2010), *op. cit.*

[348] Wright, W. C., Jr., (2002). "The Legacy of Max DePree." *Comment,* March 1, 2002 and found online on January 1, 2020 at https://www.cardus.ca/comment/article/the-legacy-of-max-de-pree/.

[349] DePree, M., (2004), *op. cit.*

[350] *Ibid.*

Unfortunately, perhaps because of the paradigms of his culture or personal philosophy, this administrator has failed to take advantage of the skills of his colleagues, has not invested in their personal development, and his chosen instead to direct his college with autocratic fiats.

The consequences of this administrator's leadership style have deprived him of the input and wisdom of his highly competent vice chancellor and other well-qualified staff. Operating under the assumption that the directives of their titular leader must always be acknowledged and supported, others have been reluctant to provide the chancellor with the advice and insights that their own experience has prepared them to contribute. The consequences for the college, its faculty, and its students are unfortunate.

Operating under the assumption that the directives of their titular leader must always be acknowledged and supported, others have been reluctant to provide him with the advice and insights that their own experience has prepared them to contribute. The consequences for the college, its faculty, and its students are unfortunate.

The school's Master of Business Administration program, sub-contracted almost entirely to a marginally-qualified United States college, delivers academic courses to students through part-time faculty who often lack adequate academic training and who are recruited just days before those visiting faculty are scheduled to teach. As a result, these visiting faculty are frequently unprepared and the school's students are neither required to purchase a text book or to read articles as part of their academic training. Although lectures are delivered in English, students have only a partial understanding of that language and the testing of student knowledge lacks rigor or validity.

Graduates of the school's academic programs **struggle to obtain employment** opportunities as they compete for jobs with graduates of other colleges and universities in the geographic area and the **reputation and prestige of the college has slowly deteriorated.**

Faculty training for full-time residential faculty is virtually non-existent and faculty rarely publish in scholarly journals. Despite opportunities to significantly upgrade student learning, improve student and faculty writing skills, and enhance the academic quality of the school's faculty, the chancellor continues to make unilateral decisions about the school. For that reason, the graduates of the school's academic programs struggle to obtain employment opportunities as they compete for jobs with graduates of other colleges and universities in the geographic area and the reputation and prestige of the college has slowly deteriorated.

The contrasting difference between the leadership style of Max DePree and that of the chancellor of this Middle East college results in a significant difference in the effectiveness of employees and in the quality of those employees' work products. DePree's commitment to developing employees led to outstanding organization success. The chancellor's unilateral and autocratic style and his failure to empowering and developing his staff and faculty have led to a decline in this college's effectiveness in the growth of the employees and in the quality of its students.

SIX PRINCIPLES FOR DEVELOPING OTHERS

As leaders examine the ways in which they can develop others and make a difference in others' lives, their efforts can not only benefit their individual employees but also strengthen the ability of their organizations to be innovative, customer-focused, and profitable[351]. The following are six well-established principles that leaders follow as they seek to develop others' highest potential.

1. Adopt a Leadership Style Focused on Service Rather Than on Position

Leaders develop others most effectively when those who follow them believe that the leaders seek to serve them, not to dominate or control them. Leadership by commitment is far more effective than leadership by control – and this point was made by Chester Barnard more than eighty years ago[352].

Leaders **develop others most effectively** when those who follow them believe that **the leaders seek to serve them, not to dominate or control** them.

Create commitment rather than just compliance!

[351] The evidence from many studies affirms that investing in employees and their growth improves the likelihood of an organization enjoying all of these benefits. See, for example, Cameron, K. S., (2013). *Practicing Positive Leadership: Tools and Techniques That Create Extraordinary Results*. San Francisco, CA: Berrett-Koehler Publishers.

[352] Barnard's position on the true nature of authority and followership were identified in Barnard, C. I., (1938). *The Functions of the Executive*. Cambridge, MA: Harvard College.

2. Treat Employees as Valued Colleagues and Full Partners

When leaders treat employees as valued partners and demonstrated high trust in them, employees are much more likely to invest in the organization, commit themselves to its goals[353], and seek to improve their ability to make the organization successful[354].

When leaders **treat employees as valued partners** and **demonstrate high trust** in them, employees are much **more likely to invest** in the organization, **commit themselves to its goals**, and seek to **improve their ability to make the organization successful**.

3. Involve Employees in Making Decisions to Develop Their Decision-Making Skills

A participative management style enables employees to not only develop their skills but to feel a sense of ownership in organizational outcomes[355]. An autocratic style that retains all of the decision-making power withholds opportunities for employees to grow and diminishes their personal ownership of an organization's goals, values, and purpose[356].

---

353 The relationship between treating employees with high trust and earning their commitment is the theme of Beer, M., (2009). *High Commitment, High Performance: How to Build a Resilient Organization for Sustained Advantage*. San Francisco, CA: Jossey-Bass.

354 Clifton, J. & Harter, J., (2019), *op. cit.*

355 Burns, J. M., (2010), *op. cit.*

356 Wyatt, S., (2020). *5 Modes of Leadership: How to Adapt Your Style to Be an Effective and Inspirational Leader*. Amherst, WI: Legend Business Press.

A participative management style **enables employees** to not only **develop their skills but to feel a sense of ownership** in organizational outcomes.

4. Make Achieving Excellence in Every Task the Ultimate Cultural Value

Excellence is the highest standard of morality and the foundation principle of every ethical perspective[357]. Creating a culture that strives to be world class is essential to success in today's competitive global economy and compromising that standard is a recipe for failure[358]. Seek to be world class and do not compromise. Leaders who hold themselves and their organization to a standard of excellence are able to create a culture that inspires employees to reach that standard[359].

Creating **a culture that strives to be world class** is essential to success in today's competitive global economy and **compromising that standard is a recipe for failure.** Seek to be world class and **do not compromise.**

[357] Robert Solomon has noted that excellence is the foundation of all ethical perspectives. See Solomon, R. C., (1992). *Ethics and Excellence: Cooperation and Integrity in Business*. New York: Oxford University Press.

[358] This simple message about the need to be world-class to succeed is an insight contained in the best-selling book, *Good to Great*. See Collins, J., (2001). *Good to Great: Why Some Companies Make the Leap . . . And Others Don't*. New York: HarperCollins.

[359] The important role of leaders in creating and sustaining organizational culture is the topic of Schein, E. H. & Schein, P. A., (2016). *Organizational Culture and Leadership* (5th ed.). Hoboken, NJ: Wiley.

5. Assist and Empower Employees as They Seek to Improve

Providing employees with opportunities to constantly learn and to develop their skills prepares those individuals to perform their roles more effectively. Employee training development is a critical part of empowering employees to enhance their potential, to contribute to achieving organizational goals, and to increase their personal commitment[360]. Employees are an investment and an asset and good employees expect to grow and will make the effort.

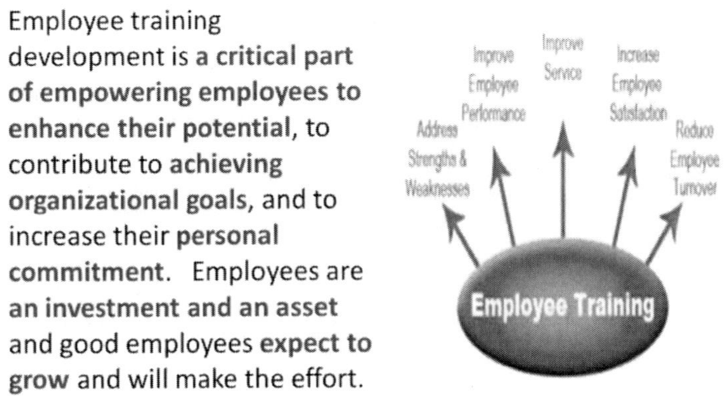

6. Treat Employees as Good as You Would Treat Your Best Customers

By valuing employees and by creating aligned systems that demonstrate the leader's commitment to employee success[361], leaders and organizations prove by their actions that there is truth to the oft-repeated words, "Our employees are our most important asset." Words are not enough. Until those

---

[360] Beer, M., (2009), *op. cit.*

[361] High performance organizations honor this principle and achieve better results than organizations that fail to demonstrate that they genuinely care about their employees. See, for example, Beer, M., (2009), *op. cit.* and Clifton, J. & Harter, J., (2019), op. cit.

words are coupled with programs, policies, and practices that genuinely treat employees as important, employees will withhold their commitment[362].

Words are not enough. Until those words are **coupled with programs, policies, and practices** that genuinely **treat employees as important,** employees will withhold their commitment.

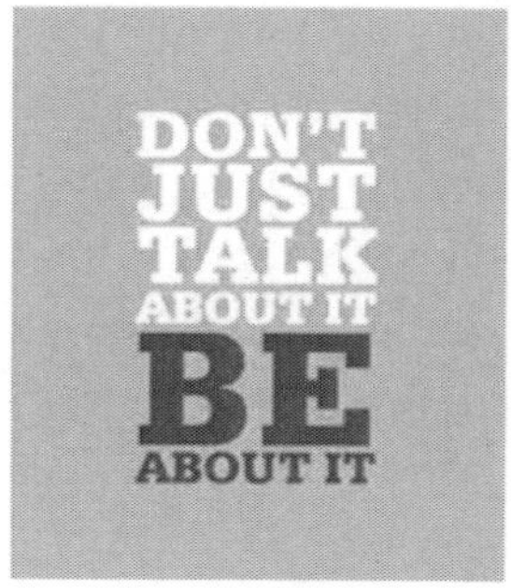

These six principles for developing others enable leaders to increase the skills of those employees whom they serve and improve their organizations – and in so doing they honor the obligation of leaders to optimize their ability to serve both the individual employees and fulfill their fiduciary responsibility in their leadership role.

Conclusion

Leadership is far more than a transactional exchange between two parties, but is a profoundly personal relationship[363]. Many who have studied leadership and its scope and responsibilities describe the leadership-employee relationship as sacred[364] and acknowledge the leader's "covenantal" obligation to serve others to help them to improve. Honoring

[362] The truth of this statement is addressed in Hayes, L., Caldwell, C., Licona, B. and Meyer, T. E., (2015). "Follower Behaviors and Barriers to Wealth Creation." *Journal of Management Development*, Vol. 34, Iss. 3, pp. 270-285 and in Pfeffer, J., (1998). *The Human Equation: Building Profits by Putting People First*. Boston, MA: Harvard Business Review Press.

[363] This insight is affirmed in countless studies about effective leadership. See Kouzes, J. M. & Posner, B. Z., (2017). *The Leadership Challenge: How to Get Extraordinary Things Done in Organizations* (6th ed.). San Francisco, CA: Jossey-Bass.

[364] Max DePree, Robert Greenleaf, Moses Pava, and Stephen R. Covey are just a few of the many leadership scholars who view leadership as a moral, personal, and sacred duty.

the leader's obligation to develop others evokes greater personal commitment from employees and benefits both the individuals served and the organizations in which they labor[365].

Honoring **the leader's obligation** to develop others **evokes greater personal commitment** from employees and **benefits both the individuals** served **and the organizations** in which they labor.

Leaders like Max DePree are truly an inspiration. Their commitment to honoring the leader's duties to others sets a standard of moral conduct and service that resonates with employees and demonstrate the virtues and the wisdom of treating employees well. The universal principles that govern relationships with others that such leaders model also confirm their practical value and the validity of the underlying truths upon which those principles are based.

Those who seek to lead others take upon themselves a **mantle of sacred responsibility** – although **many who serve** in leadership positions **fail to recognize the obligations which they assume.**

Those who seek to lead others take upon themselves a mantle of sacred responsibility – although many who serve in leadership positions fail to

---

[365] See Covey, S. R., (2004), *op. cit.*

recognize the obligations which they assume. By developing employees, by being committed to their welfare, and by encouraging their personal and professional growth, authentic leaders honor the covenantal responsibilities[366] that the highest standards of moral leadership demand[367].

[366] These covenantal responsibilities are the subject of Pava, M., (2003), *op. cit.*

[367] *Ibid*. This message about moral leadership is echoed as well by hundreds of other leadership scholars and students of optimal human interaction.

Chapter 10

LEADERSHIP AS SERVICE TO MANKIND

Robert Greenleaf, **founder of the modern servant leadership movement**, famously declared that "**(g)ood leaders must first become good servants.**"

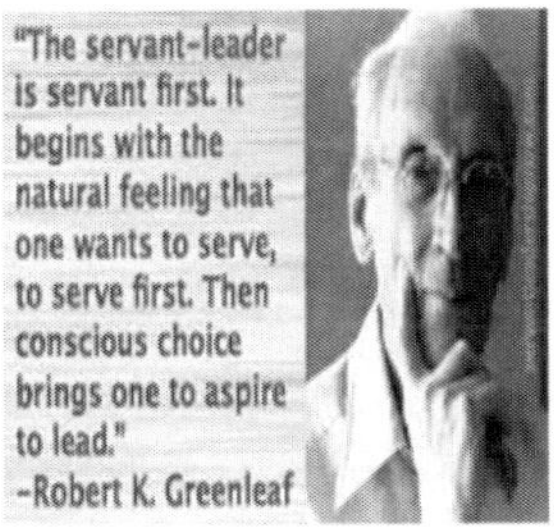

Robert Greenleaf, founder of the modern servant leadership movement, famously declared that "(g)ood leaders must first become good servants[368]." Leaders are most powerful in their contribution to the world and most respected in honoring their obligations to others when they engage in acts of meaningful service. By putting service to others above their own self-interests, leaders earn the trust of others and demonstrate their commitment to accomplishing worthy goals[369].

The purpose of this chapter is to identify the important role of service and its importance in influencing the lives of others. The chapter begins by

---

[368] "Servant Leadership Quotes." Goodreads. Found online on December 22, 2019 at https://www.goodreads.com/work/quotes/175613-servant-leadership-a-journey-into-the-nature-of-legitimate-power-and-gr.

[369] This message is the theme of Block, P., (2013). *Stewardship: Choosing Service Over Self-Interest*. San Francisco, CA: Jossey-Bass.

identifying the importance of service as a fundamental quality of great leadership. Following that summary, the chapter then identifies the consequences when leaders choose self-interest over service to others and the impacts of that choice. The chapter then describes the commitment to others and dedicated service of Dr. Roy Vagelos, former Chief Executive Officer and Chairman of Merck, Co. who was responsible for Merck developing and donating Ivermectin, a drug that cured river blindness for millions of impoverished people in the third world.

Vagelos' service to others is contrasted with the case of the individual who cornered the market on the drug, Daraprim, but who then exponentially increased the cost of that drug in a quest to line his own pocket. The chapter explains how adopting a service-oriented perspective benefits those whom a leader serves and creates value for organizations and the individuals within them. The chapter concludes with a challenge to individuals seeking to become effective leaders – encouraging them to examine their own commitment to service and their underlying assumptions about how they view leadership responsibilities.

SERVICE AND LEADERSHIP

Lao Tzu, the Chinese philosopher, observed that "(a) leader is best when people barely know he exists; when his work is done, his aim fulfilled, they will say, "We did it ourselves[370]." Servant leadership is based upon the

[370] See "Top 50 Quotes about Servant Leadership." LeadershipGeeks.com found online on December 24, 2019 at http://www.leadershipgeeks.com/servant-leadership-quotes/.

fundamental belief that by helping individual members to become their best, an organization will then reap the benefits of the leader's commitment to its employees by their reciprocating dedication to achieving the organization's goals[371].

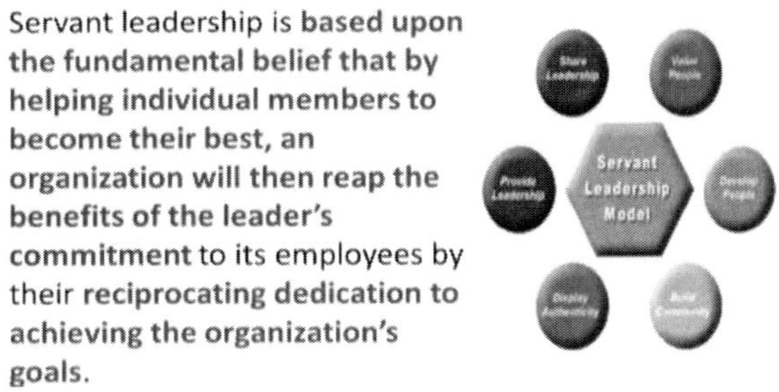

The research by Jim Collins in the highly-regarded book, *Good to Great,* confirms the importance of the understated leader as a contributor to the success of outstanding organizations[372]. Collins found that leaders who were passionately dedicated to their organization's success and who willingly gave credit to others for those successes were highly respected and optimally effective[373].

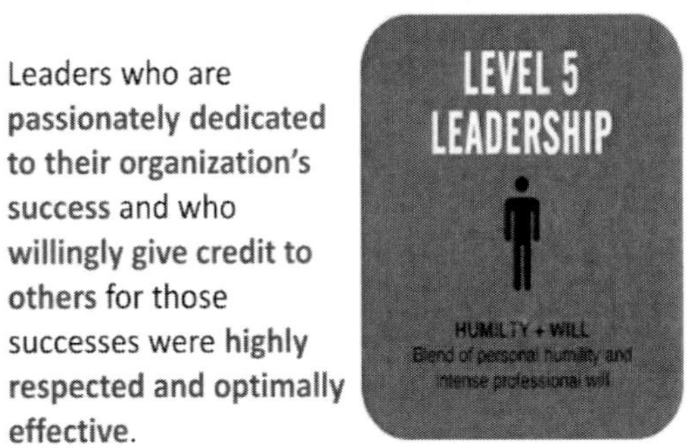

---

[371] This concept is clearly emphasized in DePree, M., (2004). *Leadership is an Art. New York*: Crown Publications.

[372] Collins, J., (2001). *Good to Great: Why Some Companies Make the Leap . . . And Others Don't.* New York: HarperCollins.

[373] *Ibid.* Collins called such leaders "Level 5 Leaders" and described them as combining humility and fierce resolve. His researchers confirmed that companies that made the transition from good to truly great were led by such individuals.

The leader's role fulfills a moral obligation to others that is based upon the assumption that leaders and organizations owe a moral responsibility that is the leader's basic obligation[374]. Leadership is a service relationship in which a leader earns the followership of others by 1) demonstrating an understanding of their commitment to shared goals and 2) providing direction in the pursuit of those goals[375]. To serve others is to assist them in the achievement of their priorities and to facilitate that achievement by providing useful resources[376]. Servant leaders take on their obligation to add value to society as a fundamental obligation of moral leadership[377].

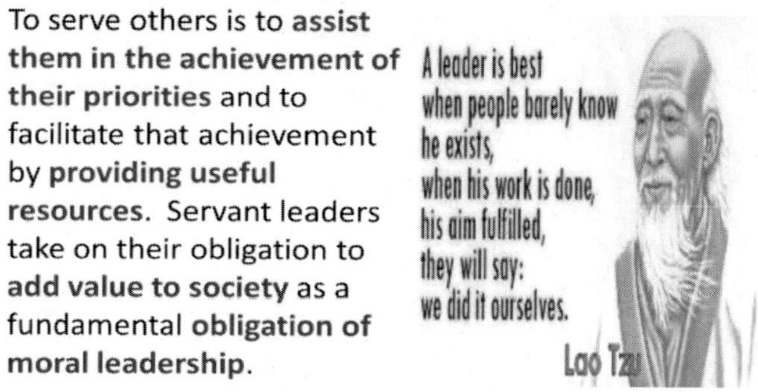

By its very nature, service to others acknowledges both others' value as individuals and the outcomes that they seek to achieve. Leaders make their most significant contribution by emphasizing "power with" others, rather than seeking to exert "power over" them[378]. Service provides a benefit that adds value or addresses an obstacle that inhibits another's ability to accomplish a desired objective. Leadership is far more an affair of the heart than an affair of the head.

---

[374] *Ibid.*

[375] This summary of leadership was articulated well in the classic book by Barnard, C. I., (1938). *The Functions of the Executive*. Cambridge, MA: Harvard College.

[376] This summary of the leader's role comes from Greenleaf, R. K. & Spears, L. C., (2002*). Servant Leadership: A Journey into the Nature of Legitimate Power and Greatness 25th Anniversary Edition*. Mahwah, NJ: Paulist Press.

[377] Block, P., (2013), *op. cit.*

[378] The principle of "power with" was articulated by the brilliant Mary Parker Follett in Follett, M. P., (2013*). Dynamic Administration: The Collected Papers of Mary Parker Follett*. Eastford, CT: Martino Fine Books.

Leaders make their most significant contribution by **emphasizing "power with"** others, rather than seeking to exert "power over" them. Service provides a benefit that **adds value or addresses an obstacle** that inhibits another's ability to accomplish a desired objective.

Leaders make a powerful contribution to others and are critical to an organization's success. In their best-selling book, *The Leadership Challenge,* James Kouzes and Barry Posner identified five specific practices that they identified as important contributors to success as leaders serve others[379].

Model the Way

Effective leaders clarify shared values and set the example by their actions. What they do is consistent with what they ask others to do. By living

---

[379] Kouzes, J. M. & Posner, B. Z., (2017). *The Leadership Challenge: How to Make Extraordinary Things Happen in Organizations* (6th ed.). San Francisco, CA: Jossey-Bass.

their values and by teaching others how to conform with those same values, they strengthen the organization.

Challenge the Process

Leaders ask appropriate questions about why organization tasks are performed in traditional ways. They search for opportunities to improve the organization and are willing to introduce better ways to achieve goals. They take well-reasoned risks and experiment when opportunities arise to improve the organization.

Inspire a Shared Vision

Leaders enlist others in the pursuit of a valued purpose and provide clear direction about worthy outcomes to achieve. They provide a clear perspective about what is possible in a way that is in harmony with shared values and ideals.

Enable Others to Act

By providing the resources and operational policies that guide employees, leaders facilitate accomplishing important tasks and guide needed changes. By establishing strong relationships, they create a climate of trust and build the confidence and competence of individual members.

Encourage the Heart

Leaders recognize the contributions of others and establish personal connection with team members. They create a spirit of community and cooperation and establish an organization culture that supports shared effort and the alignment of values.

Each of these five practices enables a leader to more effectively serve the organization, contribute to the achievement of shared goals, and benefit an organization's participants.

SELF-INTEREST: THE ANTITHESIS OF SERVANT LEADERSHIP

In contrast with the moral perspective of servant leadership, autocratic or authoritarian leadership views other individuals as a means to their own ends or as a "human resource" for the achievement of their own goals[380]. People in organizations and stakeholders outside of the organization are viewed as "Its" rather than as "Yous" – or as commodities that are to be managed to optimize efficiency, accomplish organizational goals, and promote the self-interest of the leader.

In contrast with the moral perspective of servant leadership, **autocratic or authoritarian leadership views other individuals as a means** to their own ends and as a **"human resource"** for the **achievement of their own goals.**

While servant leadership is transformational and committed to benefiting others, autocratic leadership is transactional and views the leader's responsibility as obligated only to provide a *quid pro quo* financial exchange for employees' contributions[381]. As opposed to viewing the

---

[380] "Definition of Autocratic Leadership" *The Economic Times*. Found online on December 24, 2019 at https://economictimes.indiatimes.com/definition/autocratic-leadership.

[381] The nature of transactional leadership is explained in Burns, J. M., (2010). *Leadership*. New York Harper Perennial.

leadership relationship as a personal stewardship, the autocratic leader views his or her role as being an agent pursuing outcomes that benefit his or her personal agenda. Unfortunately, many modern leaders have adopted this transactional view of employees – resulting in distrust of the leader, low organizational commitment, and mediocre individual performance.[382]

Leaders who are committed to pursuing the interests of society, optimizing long-term value creation, and serving others within the organization pursue service over self-interest and are ethical stewards.

The challenge in dealing with leaders who perceive their moral obligation as narrow is in providing incentives that benefit stakeholders long-term and optimizing long-term value creation[383]. Leaders who are committed to pursuing the interests of society, optimizing long-term value creation, and serving others within the organization pursue service over self-interest[384] and are ethical stewards[385].

ROY VAGELOS AS A SERVANT LEADER

Dr. Roy Vagelos, former Chief Executive Officer of Merck, played a major role in the development of Ivermectin, the river blindness medicine developed by Merck. River blindness, or Onchocerciasis, is a disease which

---

[382] The reality of the culture in many organizations is that employees no longer trust their leaders and are actively looking for new positions. For confirmation of this reality, see Clifton, J. & Harter, J., (2019). *It's the Manager: Gallup Finds the Quality of Managers and Team Leaders Is the Single Biggest Factor in Your Organization's Long-term Success*. Omaha, NE: Gallup Press.

[383] Caldwell, C., Hayes, L., and Long, D., (2010), *op. cit.*

[384] Block, P., (2013), *op. cit.*

[385] This distinction about the role of the leader as servant and ethical steward is found in Caldwell, C., Hayes, L., and Long, D., (2010), op. cit. and in Caldwell, C. and Anderson, V., (Eds.). (2019). *Trust, Trustworthiness, and Stewardship: A Transformative Approach*. Hauppage, New York: NOVA Publishing.

involves a parasitic worm, and is a common illness in parts of Africa, Central America, and South America[386]. Merck and Co. is a large multinational pharmaceutical company located in Kenilworth, New Jersey. Merck developed Ivermectin in 1987 – a drug originally developed to rid livestock of parasites[387] – and realized that those inflicted by river blindness were able to benefit from the drug. Those afflicted, however, were largely third-world residents that were likely to be unable to pay for the medicine[388].

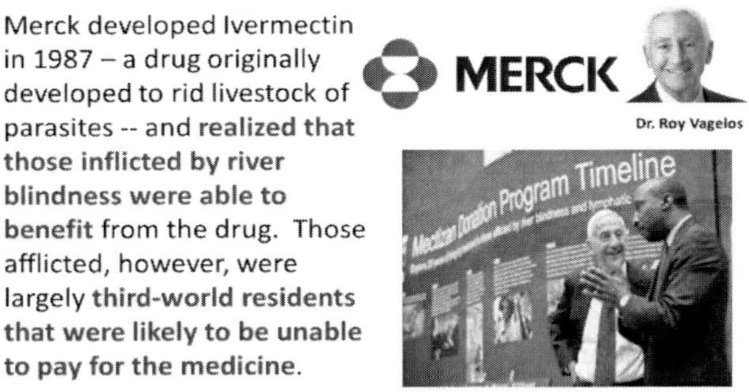

Merck's core values as articulated by their founder, George W. Merck in 1950, affirmed the commitment of their company to benefit society without concern for profit. The World Health Organization (WHO) had made the cure of river blindness a major priority[389]. From the 1970s, the WHO had struggled to develop a cure for the disease which affected more

---

386 "Global, Regional, and National Incidence, Prevalence, and Years Lived with Disability for 310 Diseases and Injuries, 1990–2015: A Systematic Analysis for the Global Burden of Disease Study 2015." (2017). Bethesda, MD: U. S. National Library of Medicine. Found online on December 24, 2019 at https://www.bing.com/maps?q=wHERE+is+the+National+Library+of+Medicine+located&form=EDNTHT&mkt=en-us&httpsmsn=1&msnews=1&plvar=0&refig=07f61831efc5497a8279d728b473a28c&PC=LCTS&sp=-1&pq=where+is+the+national+library+of+medicine+locate&sc=0-48&qs=n&sk=&cvid=07f61831efc5497a8279d728b473a28c.

387 Neill, U. S., (2014). "A Conversation with P. Roy Vagelos." *The Journal of Clinical Investigation*, Vol. 124, Iss. 6, pp. 2291-2292.

388 "Merck Offers Free Distribution of River Blindness Drug." *New York Times,* October 22, 1987 and found online on December 24, 2019 at https://www.nytimes.com/1987/10/22/world/merck-offers-free-distribution-of-new-river-blindness-drug.html.

389 "Eliminating River Blindness." World Health Organization Special Programme for Research & Training in Tropical Diseases. January 14, 2008 and found online on https://www.who.int/tdr/publications/documents/elimin_riverblind.pdf.

than 18 million people throughout the world[390]. After more than a decade of research working with several research institutions, the WHO met with Vagelos to discuss Merck's desire to produce Ivermectin. At the time, Merck had been negotiating with development and donor agencies over the purchase of ivermectin, but had received little response.

Vagelos indicated Merck's desire to make Ivermectin available to governments and health organizations at no cost to the recipients – indicating Merck's desire for the drug to make needed quantities of the drug available and put to optimum benefit for river blindness patients and others who might be at risk[391]. The impact of Vagelos' decision is summarized by the WHO report[392].

> Over the next two decades ivermectin (mectizan®) would reach over 55 million people in endemic areas of sub-Saharan Africa, with 80 million people targeted for treatment by 2015. Although not a perfect solution, annual treatment gradually brought onchocerciasis under control in most areas reached, and contributed to the elimination of onchocerciasis as a public health problem in savanna areas of West Africa.

For his actions in making the drug available, Vagelos and his successor, Dr Tore Godal, received a medal from the Prince Mahidol Award Foundation for their contributions to curing river blindness[393].

Vagelos' actions earned him and Merck Co. the **tremendous respect of people throughout the world** for their decision in **making the river blindness drug available at no cost.** Although Merck Co. recognized that it would be **foregoing substantial financial benefits** by the decision, Vagelos explained that he felt that he and his company had a **moral obligation to serve others and to benefit society.**

---

[390] *Ibid*, p. 4.
[391] *Ibid*, p. 5.
[392] *Ibid*, p. 5.
[393] *Ibid*, p. 5.

Vagelos' actions earned him and his company. the tremendous respect of people throughout the world for their decision in making the river blindness drug available at no cost. Although Merck Co. recognized that it would be foregoing substantial financial benefits by the decision, Vagelos explained that he felt that he and his company had a moral obligation to serve others and to benefit society[394].

A Leader with a Self-Interest Perspective

In marked contrast with the servant leadership of Roy Vagelos is the CEO who acquired the rights for several drugs and exponentially increased their price to consumers. In 2015, this individual and his company acquired the rights to the drug, Daraprim, and raised its price from \$13.50 per pill to \$750 per pill. Facing great public criticism, this individual defended his decision as a justifiable business decision – earning the ridicule of millions of people. Ultimately subpoenaed to appear before Congress to justify his actions, he attempted to quash the subpoena but ultimately refused to comment – citing his Fifth Amendment rights.

In marked contrast with the servant leadership of Roy Vagelos is the CEO who acquired the rights for several drugs and **exponentially increased their price to consumers**. In 2015, this individual and his company acquired the rights to the drug, Daraprim, and **raised its price from \$13.50 per pill to \$750 per pill.**

One of the clients of this fund manager ultimately sued him for \$65 million, claiming that he had breached his duty of loyalty to the company in a dispute associated with his misuse of the company's financial resources and other stock trading irregularities. After being investigated by the FBI for

[394] Neill, U. S., (2014), *op. cit.*

his actions as a financial advisor, he was charged with securities fraud and described by federal prosecutors as having been engaged in schemes to dupe investors in Ponzi-like schemes through a web of lies, deceit, and dishonesty. He was eventually indicted and convicted of two counts of securities fraud after engaging in a complex series of investment maneuvers that cost his clients millions of dollars.

After being investigated by the FBI for his actions as a financial advisor, he was **charged with securities fraud** and eventually **indicted and convicted** of two counts of securities fraud after engaging in a complex series of investment maneuvers that **cost his clients millions of dollars**.

Though described as a visionary with a brilliant intellect, this executive was also called by the media, "the most hated man in America" and "the poster child for greed." Though he appealed his conviction, an appeals court unanimously upheld his verdict and he was ordered to serve a seven-year sentence and forfeit $7.4 million in assets.

The **contrast** between the actions of Vagelos and those of his brilliant but flawed counterpart is stark and demonstrates **two extremes** in behavior, two far different perspectives about the leader's role, and two opposing attitudes about the leader's moral responsibility to others and to society. . . The profound difference in how the two leaders viewed their obligation to serve others conveys a **powerful message about leaders and leadership**.

The contrast between the actions of Vagelos and those of his brilliant but flawed counterpart is stark and demonstrates two extremes in behavior, two far different perspectives about the leader's role, and two opposing attitudes about the leader's moral responsibility to others and to society.

Both of these individuals have had a profound effect on the world around them. Both were involved in decisions about pharmaceutical drugs which had a significant impact on people's lives. Both took actions that greatly benefited individuals and society on one hand . . . or caused major problems on the other hand. The profound difference in how the two leaders viewed their obligation to serve others conveys a powerful message about leaders and leadership.

BENEFITS OF A SERVANT LEADERSHIP PERSPECTIVE

The servant leadership perspective goes **far beyond mere written words or oral statements** about an organization's priorities and values and **demonstrates by the leader's actions a far more significant commitment** to organization ideals and values.

When leaders adopt a servant leadership approach to those with whom they work, they communicate important messages to the employees with whom they work. The servant leadership perspective goes far beyond mere written words or oral statements about an organization's priorities and values and demonstrates by the leader's actions a far more significant commitment to organization ideals and values. The following are six specific benefits that leaders contribute by adopting a servant leadership perspective.

1. Affirms to Individual Organization Members That They Have the Potential and the Responsibility to Make a Significant Contribution to the Organization and to Society

By the authentic service that they render to individual employees, servant leaders communicate to organization members that they are full partners in achieving the organization's goals and that they are valued at a personal level. Servant leaders convey by their actions that they recognize the contributions that individual employees can make and that they view the leader's role as assisting employees to succeed.

Servant leaders **convey by their actions** that they **recognize the contributions** that individual employees can make and that they **view the leader's role as assisting employees** to succeed.

2. Facilitates the Ability of Others to Utilize Their Capabilities More Effectively in Accomplishing Their Own Goals

Servant leaders acknowledge that team members seek to achieve their personal goals in developing their own competencies and individual abilities. Servant leaders understand the importance of integrating individual employee capabilities and talents with the needs of the organization.

Servant leaders **acknowledge that team members seek to achieve their personal goals** in developing their own competencies and individual abilities. Servant leaders **understand the importance of integrating individual employee capabilities and talents** with the needs of the organization.

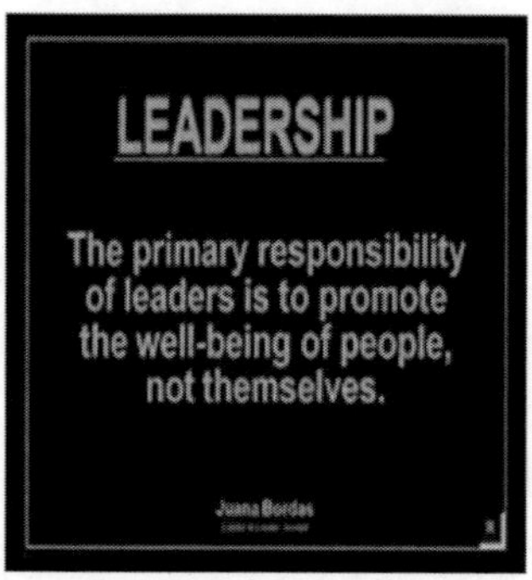

3. Demonstrates the Leader's Recognition of the Importance of Cooperation as an Implicit Value in Achieving the Organization's Purposes

By their own efforts in cooperating with and assisting employees, servant leaders model the importance of working collaboratively to optimize the organization's capabilities and to succeed in achieving its goals. Through modeling cooperative behaviors and engaging employees, servant leaders exemplify the importance of working as a team.

Through **modeling cooperative behaviors** and **engaging employees,** servant leaders **exemplify the importance of working as a team.**

4. Models the Personal Ownership, Dedication, and Commitment Expected of Members of the Organization

The **effort and energy** that servant leaders exhibit enable those leaders to be **role models of the degree of personal investment** that they are prepared to make **to benefit the organization and each individual** team member.

The effort and energy that servant leaders exhibit enable those leaders to be role models of the degree of personal investment that they are prepared to make to benefit the organization and each individual team member. Their personal example is the most effective means of communicating the leader's commitment.

5. Confirms to Individuals that They Are Valued on a Personal Level, Rather Than Viewed Simply as a Means to Achieving Organizational Goals

The effectiveness of the servant leader in treating each employee as a valued "You," or as an important individual clarifies to the entire employee group that they are valued individually and collectively – rather than being viewed as "Its," or simply a means to achieve an organizational result.

The effectiveness of the servant leader in **treating each employee as a valued "You,"** or as an important individual **clarifies to the entire employee group** that they are **valued individually and collectively**.

6. Invites Individual Team Members to Be Emotionally Engaged and Self-Empowered Contributors to the Organization's Achievements

Servant leaders have the opportunity to create a culture of engagement and empowerment by the relationships that they establish with employees and through the creation of aligned policies, programs, and practices that enable employees to be full participants in improving the organization.

Servant leaders have the opportunity to **create a culture of engagement and empowerment** by the relationships that they establish with employees and through the **creation of aligned policies, programs, and practices** that **enable employees to be full participants** in improving the organization.

These six organizational benefits assist individual employees to be more successful in accomplishing their own goals in addition to strengthening an organization's capacity to achieve its priorities. By their actions as servant leaders, those who lead honor their responsibilities owed to their organizations and its employees and also create added value to the larger community as well.

THE CHALLENGE TO LEADERS

Servant leadership is based upon the fundamental assumption that leaders have a moral duty to their organizations, their colleagues, their community, and themselves[395]. That duty is an obligation to serve others, to create long-term value for organizations, and to honor the leader's responsibility to help others to become the best version of themselves[396]. It is by serving others that leaders demonstrate their ability to contribute to the

---

[395] This moral duty is the "reality" that Max DePree explains is the first task of the leader in his outstanding book, *Leadership is an Art*. See DePree, M., (2004). *Leadership is an Art*. New York: Crown Publications.

[396] *Ibid.*

individual self-development that is essential to creating high performing organizations[397].

It is by serving others that leaders demonstrate their ability to contribute to the individual self-development that is essential to creating high performing organizations.

Those who seek to achieve personal success and organizational effectiveness must examine their own assumptions about the leader's obligations and then use that information to guide their own actions[398]. Those would-be leaders would be wise to incorporate the empirical evidence that clearly confirms that today's employees are turned off by self-serving leadership and organizations that treat them like interchangeable parts – rather than like valued partners[399].

As leaders reflect on their own lives and their own needs, they can quickly come to realize that their personal example and their commitment to serving others is ultimately how they confirm or disconfirm who they are, what they truly value, their ability to contribute to their organizations and whether they are, in fact, worthy to serve in the positions that they fill.

---

[397] See Beer, M., (2009). *High Commitment, High Performance: How to Build a Resilient Organization for Sustained Performance*. San Francisco, CA: Jossey-Bass.

[398] This assessment process requires that leaders evaluate what they know about human relationships and how leaders develop trust and employee commitment. See, for example, Caldwell & Anderson, (2019), *op. cit.*

[399] One of the outstanding summaries of the importance of treating employees well is found in Pfeffer, J., (1998). *The Human Equation: Building Profits by Putting People First*. Boston, MA: Harvard Business Review Press.

As leaders reflect on their own lives and their own needs, they can quickly come to realize that their personal example and their commitment to serving others is ultimately how they confirm or disconfirm who they are, what they truly value, their ability to contribute to their organizations and whether they are, in fact, worthy to serve in the positions that they fill.

References

Al Lawati, H. A. H., Sayed, R. T., and Caldwell, C., (2019). "Transformative Ethics and Moving Toward 'Greatness.' – Problems and Realities." *Journal of Values-Based Leadership*. Volume XII, Iss. 1, Winter/Spring Edition

Allen, S., (2018). "*The Science of Generosity*." John Templeton Foundation, .Greater Good Science Center, University of California at Berkeley found online on December 13, 2019 at https://ggsc.berkeley.edu/images/uploads/GGSC-JTF_White_Paper-Generosity-FINAL.pdf.

Anderson, V. and Caldwell, C., (Eds.).(2018). *Humility as Enlightened Leadership*. Hauppage, New York: NOVA Publishing.

Anderson, V., Caldwell, C., & Barfuss, B. 2019. "Love: The Heart of Leadership." *Graziadio Business Review,* Vol. 22, Iss. 2 and may be found online at https://gbr.pepperdine.edu/2019/08/love-the-heart-of-leadership/

Anderson, V., Ndalamba, K. K., and Caldwell, C., (2017). "Social Responsibility in a Troubled World: A Virtuous Perspective." *International Journal of Public Leadership*, Vol, 13, Iss. 2, pp 98-115.

Atwijuka, S., and Caldwell, C., (2017). "Authentic Leadership and the Ethic of Care." *Journal of Management Development*, Vol. 36, Iss. 8, pp. 1040-1051.

Audain, C., (1998). "Florence Nightingale." *Biographies of Woman Mathematicians* found online on December 21, 2019 at https://www.agnesscott.edu/lriddle/women/nitegale.htm.

Audi, R. & Murphy, P. E., (2006). *Business Ethics Quarterly*, Vol. 16, Iss. 1, pp. 3-21.

AZ Quotes. (2019). "Leadership and Change Quotes." *AZ Quotes.* Found online on December 25, 2019 at https://www.azquotes.com/quotes/topics/leadership-and-change.html.

Barnard, C. I., (1938). *The Functions of the Executive.* Cambridge, MA: Harvard College.

Baviera, T., English, W. & Guillen, M., (2016). "The 'Logic of Gift" Inspiring Behavior in Organizations Beyond the Limits of Duty and Exchange." *Business Ethics Quarterly,* Vol. 26, Iss. 2, pp. 159-180.

Beer, M., (2009). *High Commitment, High Performance: How to Build a Resilient Organization for Sustained Advantage.* San Francisco, CA: Jossey-Bass.

Bernhard, T., (2014). "20 Quotations on Generosity: A Profound Act of Kindness." *Psychology Today*, August 31, 2014 and found online on December 12, 2019 at https://www.psychologytoday.com/us/blog/turning-straw-gold/201408/20-quotations-generosity-profound-act-kindness.

Birnbaum, J., (2001). *Memorial Tributes, Volume 9 (2001).* Washington, D.C.: National Academies Press.

Block, P., (2013). *Stewardship: Choosing Service Over Self-Interest.* San Francisco, CA: Jossey-Bass.

Burke, P. J. & Stets, J. E., (2009). *Identity Theory.* Oxford, UK: Oxford University Press.

Burns, J. M., (2010). *Leadership.* New York Harper Perennial.

Caldwell, C. & Karri, R., (2019). "Leadership Morality: A Transformative Philosophy Approach." *The Journal of Business and Management,* Vol. 1, Iss. 2 and available online at https://jreslitpublications.com/business-administration-and-management/press.php,

Caldwell, C. and Anderson, V. (Eds). (2017). *Competitive Advantage: Strategies, Management, and Performance*. 2017. Hauppage, New York: NOVA Publishing.

Caldwell, C. and Anderson, V., (Eds.) (2019). *Leading with Love*. Hauppage, New York: NOVA Publishing.

Caldwell, C. and Anderson, V., (Eds.). (2019). *Trust, Trustworthiness, and Stewardship: A Transformative Approach*. Hauppage, New York: NOVA Publishing.

Caldwell, C. and Atwijuka, S.,(2019). "Self-Examination and the Ethic of Self-Interest." Paper accepted for publication in the *Journal of Values-Based Leadership.*

Caldwell, C., (2012). *Moral Leadership: A Transformative Model for Tomorrow's Leaders*. New York: Business Expert Press.

Caldwell, C., (2017). "Kindness and Self-Interest: Why Treating Employees Well Makes Such Good Sense." *Graziadio Business Review*. Vol 20, Iss. 1, found online at http://gbr.pepperdine.edu/2017/04/kindness-and-self-interest/. This citation emphasizes that kindness is a critical condition precedent for establishing the trustworthiness of a leader.

Caldwell, C., 2017. "Understanding Kindness: A Moral Duty of Human Resource Leaders." *Journal of Values-Based Leadership,* Vol. X, Iss. 2 and available online at http://scholar.valpo.edu/cgi/viewcontent.cgi?article=1188&context=jvbl.

Caldwell, C., and Dixon, R. D. (2010). "Love, Forgiveness, and Trust: Critical Values of the Modern Leader." *Journal of Business Ethics*, Vol. 93, Iss. 1, pp. 91-101.

Caldwell, C., and Floyd, L. A., (2014). "High Performance Work Systems: Building Commitment to Increase Profitability." *Graziadio Business Review*, Vol. 17, Iss. 3, found online at http://gbr.pepperdine.edu/2014/12/high-performance-work-systems/.

Caldwell, C., and Hansen, M., (2010). "Trustworthiness, Governance, and Wealth Creation." *Journal of Business Ethics*, Vol. 97, Iss. 2, pp. 173-188.

Caldwell, C., and Ndalamba, K. K., (2017). "Trust and Being 'Worthy' – The Keys to Creating Wealth." *Journal of Management Development*, Vol. 36, Iss. 8, pp. 1076-1086.

Caldwell, C., Atwijuka, S., & Okpala, C. O. (2018). "Compassionate Leadership in an Arms-Length World." *Journal of Business and Management*

Caldwell, C., Bischoff, S. J., and Karri, R. (2002). "The Four Umpires: A Paradigm for Ethical Leadership," *Journal of Business Ethics*, Vol. 36, Iss. 1/2, pp. 153-163.

Caldwell, C., Carter, E., and Floyd, L. A., (2015). "Coaching for Improved Teaching: A Virtuous Model for Improving Performance and Increasing Commitment." *Business and Management Research*, Vol. 4, No. 4, pp. 54-65.

Caldwell, C., Dixon, R. D., Floyd, L., Chaudoin, J., Post., J., and Cheokas, G. (2012). "Transformative Leadership: Achieving Unparalleled Excellence." *Journal of Business Ethics*, Vol 109, Iss. 2, pp. 175-187.

Caldwell, C., Floyd, L. A., Taylor, J and Woodard, B. (2014). "Beneficence as a Source of Competitive Advantage." *Journal of Management Development*, Vol. 33, Iss. 10, pp. 1057-1069.

Caldwell, C., Hasan, Z., and Smith, S. (2015). "Virtuous Leadership: Insights for the 21st Century." *Journal of Management Development*. Vol. 34, Iss. 9, pp. 1181-1200.

Caldwell, C., Hayes, L., and Long, D., (2010). "Leadership, Trustworthiness, and Ethical Stewardship." *Journal of Business Ethics*, Vol. 96, Iss. 4, pp. 497-512.

Caldwell, C., Hayes, L., Karri, R., and Bernal, P., (2008). "Ethical Stewardship: Implications for Leadership and Trust." *Journal of Business Ethics*, Vol. 78, Iss. 1/2, pp. 153-164.

Caldwell, C., Karri, R., & Vollmar, P., (2006). "Principal Theory and Principle Theory: Ethical Governance from the Follower's Perspective." *Journal of Business Ethics*, Vol. 66, pp. 207-223

Callahan, D., (2004). *The Cheating Culture: Why More Americans Are Doing Wrong to Get Ahead*. New York: Mariner Books.

Cameron, K. (2011). "Responsible Leadership as Virtuous Leadership." *Journal of Business Ethics*, Vol. 98, pp. 25-35.

Cameron, K. S., (2013). *Practicing Positive Leadership: Tools and Techniques That Create Extraordinary Results*. San Francisco, CA: Berrett-Koehler Publishers.

Chemers, M., (2014). *An Integrative Theory of Leadership*. London, UK: Psychology Press

Christensen, C. M., Allworth, J. & Dillon, K. (2012). *How Will You Measure Your Life?* New York: HarperCollins.

Clifton, J. & Harter, J., (2019). *It's the Manager: Gallup Finds the Quality of Managers and Team Leaders is the Single Biggest Factor in Your Organization's Long-Term Success*. Omaha, NE: Gallup Press.

Collins, J., (2001). *Good to Great: Why Some Companies Make the Leap . . . And Others Don't*. New York: HarperCollins.

Collins, J., (2003). "The 10 Greatest CEOs of All Time: What These Extraordinary Leaders Can Teach Today's Troubled Executives." *Fortune*, July 21, 2003 and found online on December 31, 2019 at https://theclci.com/wp-content/uploads/2018/03/The10GreatestCEOsOfAllTime.pdf.

Connor, T., (2018). "Who Lives in Life? Givers or Takers. The One Thing That Separates Them is Their Outlook on Life." *Personal Excellence Essentials*, Vol. 23, Iss.6, pp. 9-10.

Covey, S. R. (2004). *The 8th Habit: From Effectiveness to Greatness*. New York: Free Press, p. 98

Covey, S. R., (1992). *Principle-Centered Leadership*. New York: Fireside Press and Collins, J., (2001)

Covey, S. R., (1994). *The 7 Habits of Highly Effective People: Powerful Lessons in Personal Change*. Kottayam, Kerala, India: DC Books.

Cox, D., La Caze, M. & Levine, M. P. (2003). *Integrity and the Fragile Self*. New York: Routledge.

Crabtree, S., (2013). "Worldwide, 13% of Employees are Engaged at Work." *Gallup*. October 8, 2013 and found online on December 26, 2019 at https://news.gallup.com/poll/165269/worldwide-employees-engaged-work.aspx.

Daskal, L. "*The 100 Best Leadership Quotes of All Time*." Found online on December 27, 2019 at https://www.inc.com/lolly-daskal/the-100-best-leadership-quotes-of-all-time.html.

Davis, J. H., Schoorman, F. D. & Donaldson, L., (1997). "Toward a Stewardship Theory of Management." *Academy of Management Review*, Vol. 22, Iss. 1, pp. 20-47.

De George, R. (1993). *Competing with Integrity in International Business*. New York: Oxford University Press

Deming, W. E., (2000). *Out of the Crisis*. Cambridge, MA: MIT Press.

DePree, M., (2004). *Leadership is an Art*. New York: Crown Publications.

DeTienne, K. B., Ellertson, C. F., Ingerson, M-C. & Dudley, W. R., (2019). "Moral Development in Business Ethics: An Examination and Critique." *Journal of Business Ethics.*

Dill, K., (2014). "The End of 'Macho'? Survey Identifies Feminine Leadership Communication as the Way of the Future." *Forbes.com*, p. 21, May 20, 2014 and found online on December 18, 2019 at https://www.forbes.com/sites/kathryndill/2014/05/20/the-end-of-macho-survey-identifies-feminine-leadership-communication-as-the-way-of-the-future/#76bdb8aa5b4d.

Firestone, L., (2010). "Generosity: What's In It for You?" *Psychology Today*, November 24, 2010 and found online on December 13, 2019 at https://ggsc.berkeley.edu/images/uploads/GGSC-JTF_White_Paper-Generosity-FINAL.pdf

Follett, M. P., (2013*). Dynamic Administration: The Collected Papers of Mary Parker Follett*. Eastford, CT: Martino Fine Books.

Freeman, R. E. (1984). *Strategic Management: A Stakeholder Approach*. New York: Cambridge University Press.

Friedman, M., (1970). "The Social Responsibility of Business is to Increase its Profits." *New York Times Magazine.* Found online on December 30, 2019 at http://www.umich.edu/~thecore/doc/Friedman.pdf.

Friedman, T. L., (2009*). Hot, Flat, and Crowded: Why We Need a Green Revolution – And How It Can Renew America, Release 2.0*. New York: Picador Press.

Fromm, E., (2006). *The Art of Loving*. New York: Harper Perennial.

Gates, D., (2017). "*Self-Interest, Ethics, and Success*." BYU Wheatley Institution, September 26, 2017 and found online on November 30, 2019 at https://wheatley.byu.edu/self-interest-ethics-and-success/.

George, B., (2004). *Authentic Leadership: Rediscovering the Secrets to Creating Lasting Value*. San Francisco, CA: Jossey-Bass.

Gilligan, C., (2016). *In a Different Voice: Psychological Theory and Women's Development*. Boston, MA: Harvard University Press.

Glint research report, "The State of Employee Engagement in 2019." *HR.com*, p. 5-6.

Goler, L, Gale, J., Harrington, B. & Grant A., (2018). "Why People Really Quit Their Jobs." *Harvard Business Review*, January 11, 2018, and found online on December 15, 2019 at https://hbr.org/2018/01/why-people-really-quit-their-jobs.

Goodreads (2019). "Florence Nightingale Quotes." *Goodreads*. Found online on December 21, 2019 at https://www.goodreads.com/author/quotes/63031.Florence_Nightingale.

Gray, C., (2019). "It's a Man's World . . .Or Is It? Finding a Seat at the Table for Feminine Leadership." *Leadership Excellence*, Vol. 36, Iss. 9, pp. 5-7.

Greenleaf, R. K. & Spears, L. C., (2002). *Servant Leadership: A Journey into the Nature of Legitimate Power and Greatness 25th Anniversary Edition*. Mahwah, NJ: Paulist Press.

Hamilton, L. M. & North, W. (2015). *Florence Nightingale: A Life Inspired*. Sudbury, MA: Wyatt North Publishing.

Harrington, M., (2017). "Survey: Peoples Trust has Declined in Business, Media, Government, and NGOs." *Harvard Business Review*, January 16, 2017 and found online on December 27, 2019 at https://hbr.org/2017/01/survey-peoples-trust-has-declined-in-business-media-government-and-ngos.

Hayes, L., Caldwell, C., Licona, B. and Meyer, T. E., (2015). "Follower Behaviors and Barriers to Wealth Creation." *Journal of Management Development*, Vol. 34, Iss. 3, pp. 270-285.

Hernandez, M., (2008). "Promoting Stewardship Behavior in Organizations: A Leadership Model." *Journal of Business Ethics*, Vol. 80, Iss. 1, pp. 121-128,

Hosmer, L. T., (1995). "Trust: The Connecting Link Between Organizational Theory and Philosophical Ethics." *Academy of Management Review*, Vol. 20, Iss. 2, pp. 379-403

Huntsman, J. M. Sr., (2008). *Winners Never Cheat: Even in Difficult Times, New and Expanded Version*. Hoboken, NJ: Pearson FT Press.

Huntsman, J., Sr., (2014). *Barefoot to Billionaire: Reflections on a Life's Work and a Promise to Cure Cancer*. New York: Harry N. Abrams Publishers.

Inagaki, T. E. & Ross, L. P., (2018). "*Neural Correlates of Giving Social Support: Differences Between Giving Targeted and Untargeted Support*." Preprint found on December 13, 2019 at https://psyarxiv.com/eudqf/

Jironet, K. (2019). *Feminine Leadership: Personal Development Beyond Polarities*. New York: Routledge.

Johnson, B., (2018). "Jon Huntsman, Sr. Passes Away." *BlockU.com*, February 2, 2018 and found online on December 8, 2019 at https://www.blocku.com/2018/2/2/16966998/jon-huntsman-sr-passes-away.

Jung, C. G., (2006). *The Undiscovered Self: The Dilemma of the Individual in Modern Society*. New York:

Kets de Vries, M. F. R. & Miller, D., (1991). *The Neurotic Organization: Diagnosing and Revitalizing Unhealthy Companies* (2nd ed.). New York: HarperCollins.

Kohlberg, L., (1981). *The Philosophy of Moral Development: Moral Stages and the Idea of Justice*. New York: Harper and Row.

Kotter J.P. & Schlesinger L.A. (1989) "Choosing Strategies for Change" in D. Asch & C. Bowman (Eds.) *Readings in Strategic Management*. London: Palgrave Macmillan, pp. 294-306.

Kotter, J. P., (2012). *Leading Change, With a New Preface by the Author*. Boston, MA: Harvard Business Review Press.

Kouzes, J. M. & Posner, B. Z. (2017). *The Leadership Challenge: How to Make Extraordinary Things Happen in Organizations.* San Francisco, CA: Jossey-Bass.

Kouzes, J. M. & Posner, B. Z., (2011). *Credibility: How Leaders Gain and Lose It, Why People Demand It.* San Francisco, CA: Jossey-Bass.

Kouzes, J. M. & Posner, B. Z., (2017). *The Leadership Challenge: How to Make Extraordinary Things Happen in Organizations* (6th ed.). San Francisco, CA: Jossey-Bass.

Lee, H., (2005). *To Kill a Mockingbird.* New York: Harper Perennial.

Lennick, D. & Kiel, F., (2011). *Moral Intelligence 2.0: Enhancing Business Performance and Leadership Success in Turbulent Times.* Upper Saddle River, NJ: FT Press.

Leung, R., (2003). "The Mensch of Malden Mills." *CBS News 60 Minutes*, July 2003 and found online on December 6, 2019 at https://www.cbsnews.com/news/the-mensch.

Lewis, C. S. & Norris, K., (2015). *Mere Christianity.* New York: Harper One

Lewis, J. J., (2019). "The Glass Ceiling and Women's History: An Invisible Barrier to Success," *ThoughtCo.*, August 18, 2019 and found online on December 17, 2019 at https://www.thoughtco.com/glass-ceiling-for-women-definition-3530823.

Lock, S., (2019). "System Sales of Chick-fil-A in the United States from 2016 to 2018."*Statista*, August 13, 2019 and found online on December 16, 2019 at https://www.statista.com/statistics/743343/system-sales-of-chick-fil-a/.

Loden, M., (1986). "Feminine Leadership: It Can Make Your Business More Profitable." *Vital Speeches of the Day*, Vol. 52, Iss. 15, pp. 472-473. Delivered at the Baltimore Business Leader Conference, Notre Dame College, Baltimore, Maryland, March 13, 1986.

London, M., (2014). *The Power of Feedback.* New York: Routledge.

Love, A., (2018). "Leveraging the Power of Feminine Leadership." *PA Times*, Vol. 4, Iss. 2, pp. 37-38.

Manville, B. & Ober, J., (2003). *A Company of Citizens: What the World's First Democracy Teaches Leaders About Creating Great Organizations*. Boston, MA: Harvard Business Review Press.

Mayer, R. C., Davis, J. H. & Schoorman, F. D., (1995). "An Integrative Model of Organizational Trust." *Academy of Management Review*, Vol. 20, No. 3, pp. 709-734.

Maze., J., (2018). "When It Comes to Reputation, Chick-fil-A is King." *Restaurant Business Online*, March 22, 2018 and found online on December 16, 2019 at https://www.restaurantbusinessonline.com/marketing/when-it-comes-reputation-chick-fil-king

Mead, A. (N.D.). "30 Inspirational Quotes on Integrity." *Awaken the Greatness Within*. Found online on December 10, 2019 at https://www.awakenthegreatnesswithin.com/30-inspirational-quotes-on-integrity/.

Moreno, K., (2003). "Trial by Fire." *Forbes*, April 14, 2003 and found online on December 6, 2019 at https://www.forbes.com/forbes/2003/0414/092.html#3fa8ec4b6391.

Moynihan, D. P., DeLeire, T., & Kohei, E., (2013). "A Life Worth Living: Evidence on the Relationship Between Prosocial Values and Happiness." Found online on December 13, 2019 at https://pdfs.semanticscholar.org/1d7f/30c6f99ad400579fe24eac4c3cdfefdcd7c8.pdf?_ga=2.79721879.1693506563.1576256574-1463184506.1576256574 and published in the *American Review of Public Administration* in 2015.

Munro, I. & Thanem, T., (2018). "The Ethics of Affective Leadership: Organizing Good Encounters Without Leaders." *Business Ethics Quarterly*, Vol. 28, Iss. 1, pp. 51-69.

Neill, U. S., (2014). "A Conversation with P. Roy Vagelos." *The Journal of Clinical Investigation*, Vol. 124, Iss. 6, pp. 2291-2292.

New York Times. (2019). "Merck Offers Free Distribution of River Blindness Drug." *New York Times,* October 22, 1987 and found online on December 24, 2019 at https://www.nytimes.com/1987/10/22/world/merck-offers-free-distribution-of-new-river-blindness-drug.html.

Notre Dame University "*Science of Generosity*" project found online on December 13, 2019 at https://generosityresearch.nd.edu/.

Nulty, P & Llosa, P., (1992). "The National Business Hall of Fame". *Fortune,* Vol. 125, Issue 6, March 23, 1992.

Okpala, C. O. & Caldwell, C. (2019). "Humility, Forgiveness, and Love: The Heart of Ethical Stewardship." *Journal of Values-Based Leadership*, Vol. 12 Summer 2019 and found online at https://scholar.valpo.edu/jvbl/vol12/iss2/10/

Packard, D. (2006). *The HP Way: How Bill Hewlett and I Built Our Company*. New York: HarperCollins.

Paine, L. S., (1997). "Integrity." In *The Blackwell Encyclopedic Dictionary of Business Ethics*, Werhane, P H.

Paris, L. D., Howell, J. P, Dorfman, P. W. & Hanges, P. J., (2009). "Preferred Leadership Prototypes of Male and Female Leaders in 27 Countries." *Journal of International Business Studies*, Vol. 40, pp. 1396–1405

Pava, M., (2003). *Leading with Meaning: Using Covenantal Leadership to Build a Better Organization*. New York: St. Martin's Press.

Pfeffer, J., (1998). *The Human Equation: Building Profit by Putting People First*. Boston, MA: Harvard Business Review Press.

Pollack, J., Pollack, R. (2014). "Using Kotter's Eight Stage Process to Manage an Organisational Change Program: Presentation and Practice." *Systemic Practice and Action Research*, Vol. 28, pp. 51-66.

Ramsey, D. (2019). "7 Life Lessons from Truett Cathy." *Dave Ramsey.com* found online on December 16, 2019 at https://www.daveramsey.com/blog/7-life-lessons-from-truett-cathy.

Ritchie, G. D., Still, K. R., Alexander, W. K.; Nordholm, A. F,; Wilson, C. L.,Rossi, J., & Mattie, D. R. (2001). "A Review of the Neurotoxicity Risk of selected Hydrocarbon Fuels". *Journal of Toxicology and Environmental Health. Part B, Critical Reviews*, Volume 4, No. 3, pp.: 223–312

Rousseau, D. M., (1995). *Psychological Contracts in Organizations: Understanding Written and Unwritten Agreements*. Thousand Oaks, CA: Sage Publications.

Schein, E. H. & Schein, P. A., (2016). *Organizational Culture and Leadership* (5th ed.). Hoboken, NJ: Wiley.

Scholtes, P. R., Joiner, B. L. & Streibel, B. J., (2018). *The TEAM Handbook* (3rd ed.). Hooksett, NH: Goal/QPC.

Senge, P. M., (2006). *The Fifth Discipline: The Art & Practice of the Learning Organization* (2nd ed.). New York: Doubleday.

Signet and Caldwell, C., (2000). *Communication, Meaning, and Identity: Moving Toward Discovery*. Hauppage, NY: NOVA Publishing.

Smircich, L. & Morgan, (1982). 'Leadership: The Management of Meaning." *Journal of Applied Behavioral Science*, Vol. 18, No. 3, pp. 257-273

Smith, A., (1759). *The Theory of Moral Sentiments*. London and Edinburgh, UK: A. Strahan; and T. Cadell, in the Strand; and T. Creech and J. Bell & Co. at Edinburgh.

Smith, C. & Davidson, H. (2014). *The Paradox of Generosity*. New York: Oxford University Press.

Solomon, R. C., (1992). *Ethics and Excellence: Cooperation and Integrity in Business*. New York: Oxford University Press.

Soltes, E., (20109). "Where is Your Company Most Prone to Lapses in Integrity?" *Harvard Business Review*, Vol. 97, Iss. 4, pp. 51-54.

Straczynski, S., (2010). "Herman Miller Named 'Most Admired' Company" *Contract Design Network*, March 8, 2010 and found online on January 1, 2020 at https://www.contractdesign.com/news/main/herman-miller-namedmost-admired-company/.

Sudbrink, L., (2016) "Leveraging GRIT for Leadership Success." *Leader to Leader*, Vol. 2016, Iss. 79, pp. 57-62.

Tannen, D., (2007). *You Just Don't Understand: Women and Men in Conversation*. New York: HarperCollins.

US National Library of Medicine. (2017). "*Global, Regional, and National Incidence, Prevalence, and Years Lived with Disability for 310 Diseases and Injuries, 1990–2015: A Systematic Analysis for the Global Burden of Disease Study 2015*." (2017). Bethesda, MD: U. S. National Library of Medicine. Found online on December 24, 2019 at https://www.bing.com/maps?q=wHERE+is+the+National+Library+of

+Medicine+located&form=EDNTHT&mkt=en-us&httpsmsn=1&msnews=1&plvar=0&refig=07f61831efc5497a8279d728b473a28c&PC=LCTS&sp=-1&pq=where+is+the+national+library+of+medicine+locate&sc=0-48&qs=n&sk=&cvid=07f61831efc5497a8279d728b473a28c.

Whalen, P., (2019). "Goldman Sachs and the ABACUS Deal." *Seven Pillars Institute*. Kansas City, MO. Found online on December 15, 2019 at https://sevenpillarsinstitute.org/case-studies/goldman-sachs-and-the-abacus-deal/.

Wharton School, (2018). "*Remembering Jon M. Huntsman, Sr.: Lessons from a Compassionate Leader*." University of Pennsylvania February 6, 2018 and found online on December 9, 2018 at https://knowledge.wharton.upenn.edu/article/remembering-jon-m-huntsman-sr-lessons-compassionate-leader/.

Whitmore, J., (2017). *Coaching for Improved Performance: The Principles and Practices of Coaching and Leadership* (5th ed.). Boston, MA: Nicholas Brealey Publishing.

Williamson, M., (1996). *A Return to Love: Reflections on the Principles of "A Course in Miracles."* New York: Harper One.

World Health Organization. (2008). "Eliminating River Blindness." *World Health Organization Special Programme for Research & Training in Tropical Diseases*. January 14, 2008 and found online on https://www.who.int/tdr/publications/documents/elimin_riverblind.pdf.

Wright, W. C., Jr., (2002). "The Legacy of Max DePree." *Comment,* March 1, 2002 and found online on January 1, 2020 at https://www.cardus.ca/comment/article/the-legacy-of-max-de-pree/.

Wyatt, S., (2020). *5 Modes of Leadership: How to Adapt Your Style to Be an Effective and Inspirational Leader*. Amherst, WI: Legend Business Press.

Yang, F., Liu, J., Wang, Z. & Zhang, Y., (2019). "*Feeling Energized: A Multilevel Model of Spiritual Leadership, Leader Integrity*",

Yunus, M. (2011). *Building Social Business: The New Kind of Capitalism that Serves Humanity's Most Pressing Needs*. Philadelphia, PA: Perseus Books.

Yunus, M., (2008). *Banker to the Poor: Micro-Lending and the Battle Against World Poverty*. Philadelphia, PA: Perseus Books.

About the Authors

Dr. Cam Caldwell
Business Professor, Retired
Email: cam.caldwell@gmail.com

Dr. Cam Caldwell received his PhD in Human Resources and Organization Behavior from Washington State University where he was a Thomas S. Foley Graduate Fellow. He holds the Senior Professional and Global Professional in Human Resources professional certifications. Prior to earning his PhD, he worked as a Human Resource Director, City Manager, and Management Consultant for more than twenty years. This is his tenth book and he has published many papers about a variety of management and leadership topics.

Dr. Verl Anderson
Business Professor
Dixie State University
Email: verl@dixie.edu

Dr. Verl Anderson obtained his doctorate degree in Business Administration from Arizona State University. He is currently a professor in Management and International Business at Dixie State University, St George, Utah. He has taught university courses as a visiting professor in New Zealand and four universities in China. He has published 34 articles in the past two years on leadership, ethics, China culture, kindness, strategic management, and social responsibility. His research interests include China culture and international cultures. He has traveled extensively, and annually takes groups on cultural/educational tours to China and New Zealand.

INDEX

J

K

L

M

N

O

P

R

S

T

U

V

W